W9-BCV-999

DEC 1 5 2008

9-18 (14)

I Still Have It . . .
I Just Can't Remember
Where I Put It

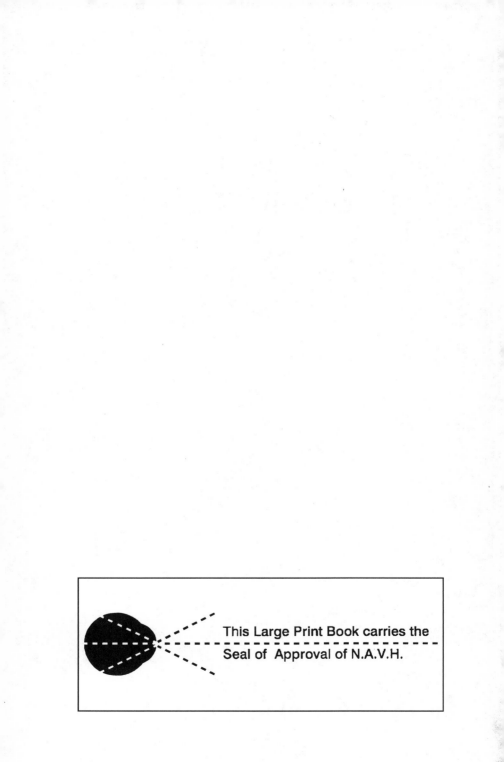

This Large Print Book carries the
Seal of Approval of N.A.V.H.

I STILL HAVE IT . . .
I JUST CAN'T REMEMBER
WHERE I PUT IT

CONFESSIONS OF A FIFTYSOMETHING

RITA RUDNER

THORNDIKE PRESS
A part of Gale, Cengage Learning

GALE
CENGAGE Learning™

Detroit • New York • San Francisco • New Haven, Conn • Waterville, Maine • London

GALE
CENGAGE Learning™

LIBRARY OF CONGRESS CATALOGING-IN-PUBLICATION DATA

Rudner, Rita.
    I still have it—I just can't remember where I put it :
confessions of a fiftysomething / By Rita Rudner.
    p. cm. — (Thorndike Press large print laugh lines)
    ISBN-13: 978-1-4104-1119-8 (hardcover : alk. paper)
    ISBN-10: 1-4104-1119-2 (hardcover : alk. paper)
    1. American wit and humor. 2. Large type books. I. Title.
PN6165.R83 2008b
818'.5402—dc22   2008034657

Published in 2008 by arrangement with Crown Publishers, a division of
Random House, Inc.

Printed in the United States of America
1 2 3 4 5 6 7 12 11 10 09 08

*For my lovely daughter, Molly,
who got old enough to go to school
so I could finish this book.*

CONTENTS

I Can't Believe I'm Filthy 11
Catalogue Addiction 13
Do It Again 22
Oh, Mother! 27
Go Ahead, Open This Bag 33
Future Reality Shows 37
A Hole in Eight 39
At What Price? 47
CNNNMSNBCCNBC
      FOXNEWSNETWORK
      HEADLINENEWS
      LOCALANDNATIONAL
      NEWS 52
And Away It Went 58
And the Gift Basket Goes To 67
And Up 73
Casualties 79
Christmas Rap 85
Superficial Nightmares of the
      Overprivileged Woman 91
Dining in the Dark 93
Drive-By Hooting 101

Everything New Is Old Again 108
Things That Amaze Me 113
Fishy Friends 114
Ginboree 121
Father Days 128
'Twas the Night After Christmas . . 136
If Not Now, When? 138
It's My Daughter's Party and
    I'll Cry if I Want To 146
The Knee-Jerk No 152
Overpaying Your Dues 160
The Second Act 166
On Your Mark, Get Set, Sit Down . . 175
Things That Palpably Don't Work . . 181
Please Don't Be My Neighbor . . . 182
Vacations of the Not So Rich
    and Famous 190
What to Wear . . . Not 199
Things I Never Thought I Would
    See in My Lifetime 204
Television Envy 205
The Abbreviation Generation . . . 213
The Advantage of Vintage 218
The Proof Is in the Child 224
The Pillow Show 231
The Scan 236
It's My Potty and I'll Cry
    If I Want To 243
To Hell in a Handbag 250
Undercover Wear 259
Speak Up 266
Shake, Rattle, and Rebuild 273

Who Don't You Trust?. 280
My Dog Bonkers. 286
Endgame 296
    ACKNOWLEDGMENTS 299

I Can't Believe I'm Filthy

There is something so traumatic about a woman turning fifty that for a while I was unable to form the actual word. I was more comfortable getting a laugh and telling people I was filthy than having to say the word *fffifffffty.* In fact, I still stutter a bit, even in print. Half a century is a long time to be on the planet, and though I'm grateful to be not only alive but healthy, being healthy gives you the freedom to obsess over the things that don't really matter, like wrinkles, veins, and how tricky it is these days just to be able to turn on — excuse me, I mean power up — a television.

I feel that life is broken down into these stages: you're born and you don't know how anything works; gradually you find out how everything works; technology evolves and slowly there are a few things you can't work; at the end, you don't know how anything works.

With the passing of every decade, our mortality becomes a little clearer and our eyesight a little fuzzier. One day the writing on the menu becomes so blurry you just can't bluff anymore. Now, I have to mention that in this optical respect, I'm lucky. I can see close up and my husband can see far away, so we're covered. He tells me who's in the movie and I tell him what's in his sandwich. Together we're human bifocals.

The comforting factor about age is that nobody is immune. The blond-haired bombshells of today are the blue-haired ladies of tomorrow. When I turned fifty, it also gave me cause to reflect on all the things that have gone right in my life. Marrying the right man, choosing the right career, and making sure my closet had lots of hanging space were all good decisions.

Fifty also caused me to reflect on friends who have left me too early due to genetics, disease, or simply being in the wrong place at the wrong time. I hope I'm lucky enough to live until I'm totally incontinent — I mean incompetent. In the meantime, I'm determined to enjoy and celebrate everything about being in my filthies.

CATALOGUE
ADDICTION

While I do occasionally order items on the Internet, it's hard to teach an old shopper new tricks. I'm convinced that the catalogue will eventually disappear, but not until the last baby boomers have kicked off their smelly Nikes and been buried in mulch.

There is currently no treatment center in Malibu for catalogue addiction, so I was forced to assemble a group of women with similar problems to meet in my living room. They all had room to sit once I moved some catalogues.

I blame Victoria's Secret. My friend ordered a blouse for me as a birthday present, and the company's first final clearance catalogue made its way into my clutches three houses ago. It doesn't matter how often I move; the catalogue knows where I'm living. If I'm ever kidnapped, I'm certain it would find me before the police.

After perusing the final clearance issue

numerous times and folding down the corners of pages showing outfits that were in the running but had not yet won my love, I ordered a pink sweatshirt and matching sweatpants. Since then, I have received roughly three hundred catalogues featuring buxom babes clad in scanty attire. On page 27 you can still find the same pink sweatsuit I ordered ten years ago. Either I am the only woman in the world who likes pink sweatsuits or they dramatically overstock — or possibly they just like the picture.

Now, I love the Victoria's Secret catalogue, but I have to mention that with each issue it edges closer and closer to pornography. The bosoms on the otherwise skinny women appear to be inflated. The last issue was so chockfull of overly endowed ladies, I couldn't even keep the magazine closed. And where exactly would I wear a head-to-toe black lace jumpsuit? At a Peeping Tom convention? Plus, as far as I know, there are only two types of women who prefer garter belts and stockings to panty hose: hookers and my mother-in-law. Hookers because of obvious reasons, and my mother-in-law because of her unwillingness to acknowledge the existence of any stocking advancements since 1947.

The Victoria's Secret catalogue was only

the tip of my problem. If that were the only booklet I was receiving, my mailman would not be in the hospital with a hernia. Word instantly goes out into the catalogue universe if you order so much as a pen, and the next day your mailbox is stuffed with a cornucopia of nonsense.

It was last November that I first noticed Herb exiting from his mail truck rather delicately as he lifted the block of catalogues too thick to be placed in my mailbox and dropped them on the ground like firewood.

"I think this might be my last holiday season delivery," he said. "My lumbar support belt isn't really cutting it anymore."

"Is it me? Is it my catalogues?" I asked guiltily.

"It's not just you," he reassured me. "It's all women . . . and Neiman Marcus."

"Is it the BOOK?" I belched.

"Yes, the BOOK is here. I have the BOOK."

"Is it in that stack of crap? You don't put the BOOK in a stack of crap," I said, pointing to the roped-together periodicals.

"No, I separated it. It was too heavy."

Herb then handed me the BOOK. If you are not familiar with the BOOK, every Christmas Neiman Marcus puts out a BOOK of things that people can't possibly afford. It's beautiful, it's classy, and last year it featured a space station that cost several million dollars. I took it from Herb and caressed it with my nearsighted eyes.

Herb then handed me seven catalogues from Pottery Barn.

"Can I ask you something?" Herb mumbled wearily.

"Sure," I replied, folding down a corner of a page of the BOOK featuring a belt costing 65,000 dollars.

"Why do you need seven catalogues that are exactly the same?"

"If you look closely, they're not all exactly the same. My name is spelled slightly differently on every single copy. The computer made a mistake and there is no going back."

"So when they come next time, can I throw away five of them?"

"What? Are you mad? They're a family. When I throw them away, I want them to be together."

The really sad thing is that I haven't ordered anything from Pottery Barn for over six years. But you never know . . . someday a lamp, a bed frame, and a bureau just might catch my eye and we could be together for the rest of our lives.

It was then that I spotted Herb holding the new Williams-Sonoma, or as my mother-in-law calls it, Williams and Sonoma. She might be right. It has to take at least two people to think up that many things nobody needs.

"Give that to me," I commanded.

"Don't grab," Herb scolded, pulling it away. "Your husband promised me a big Christmas tip if I didn't let you have this."

"I'll give you a bigger one if you give it to me," I replied, ripping it out of his hands.

"Please don't sign me up for the cheese-of-the-month club again. I can't take it," Herb pleaded. "Nobody could eat that much cheese. Mickey Mouse would have given up on it."

"You didn't like my cheese gift?" I asked in horror. "It cost two hundred and twenty dollars plus shipping."

"I like cheese. But if I run out, I can drive to the supermarket and buy some more."

"But this cheese comes in the mail."

"Rita, I'm a mailman. That sort of thing doesn't impress me."

I flicked through the catalogue.

"What about a pigeon toaster? It has a specific heat designed only for toasting pigeons. . . . Or maybe a cake girdle. If your cake is too big for the plate, you can squeeze it and correct the size. . . . Or maybe a turkey shredder. If you've cooked a bad turkey and you don't want anyone to know, you can shred it."

When I looked up, Herb had already gone. I never saw him again, and I know that wherever he is, he's in a happier place.

My husband tried to help me in any way he could. He would make an effort to be the first one to our mailbox and throw the filthy paper temptresses away before I could see them.

"I'm only doing this for you," he would say, trying to save me and my credit card from myself.

I'm not proud of this, but I would actually dig in our garbage, fish out the discarded beauties, and dry their coffee-stained pages in the sun. It wasn't even that I needed to order anything; it was that I had to see what was available to me, just in case.

I feel the reason catalogue shopping has not lessened with the advent of the Internet is the limited but crucial social contact that you get to enjoy with people over the phone. It's like talking to a relative that you never have to see. I like speaking to people who are doing their best to be polite to me. I like giving my source code and my customer number, which appears in the little blue box on the back of the catalogue. I like that the call is being recorded to ensure impeccable and courteous behavior.

"Hi, this is Betty. How can I help you?"

I picture a friendly white-haired lady in her sixties wearing her glasses on a chain around her neck. She has a picture of her grandchildren on her desk as she writes down my order longhand.

Ordering on the Internet, I picture a badly dressed teenager with greasy hair in a warehouse examining a crumpled piece of paper, climbing up a ladder, matching the number to a box, and then tossing the box into an anonymous receptacle below. It's just not the same.

I've kept my biggest difficulty with catalogues from you until now. It's not so much the ordering that's the problem as it is my inability to throw the little suckers away. I didn't know how many I possessed, but they were hidden everywhere: under the side table next to my bed, behind curtains, and yes, even in my daughter's bedroom. I'm so ashamed.

They are all gone now. I had a group of women from my meetings come over and we burned them in the backyard. Oh, they still come in the mail. There is no way to stop that. But now I look at them and throw them away, if not immediately, then certainly the next day. If I feel the need to hide one, I call my sponsor and she stays on the line until I agree to smear it with ketchup and throw it in the garbage.

I recognize that I have a problem, but I'm in recovery. I must be, because I recently received my first recovery catalogue.

When you get older, you really appreciate sleep. It's the best of both worlds: you get to be alive and unconscious.

Do It Again

Because I was a child such a very long time ago and my contact with children until I had my own was so limited, I was entirely unaware of a child's capacity for repetition.

In a typical hide-and-seek session it is not unusual for my child to hide in the same place fifteen times. I've tried to explain it to her.

"Molly, the whole idea of hide-and-seek is to vary the places that you hide so I can't find you. Do you understand?"

"Yes, Mommy. You tell me a new place to hide and I'll hide there."

"Excellent. I'm glad I've gotten my point across."

Instead of hiding behind the bookcase, she'll hide in the new place I picked out. Upon finding her, she squeals in delight and shouts, "Do it again."

A while ago I made the mistake of carrying my daughter to her bath upside down.

She is almost five years old and weighs forty pounds. I know it was in my power to say no and not carry her to the bath upside down ten times, but she is very persuasive.

"Just one more time, Mommy, I promise, this is the very last time. Really, it is. Mommy, just once. Really."

I hauled her upside down and proceeded to jog to the bathroom holding my forty-pound weight, reversed her, and placed her carefully down on the bathroom rug.

"OK, now it's time for your bath."

"Do it again, just one more time. I promise. This is the last time. Really, really, really."

And I would believe her, just like a first-time home builder being told by a general contractor, "I swear, I will not go over budget."

In our third hour of playing on the beach one day, my daughter actually got tired of building sand castles and knocking them down and we decided to go for a walk and look for seashells. This is harder than it sounds. I don't know where you live or if you've been to the beach lately, but there is a severe shortage of seashells. There are plenty of bottle caps, plastic forks, and the odd unmentionable decorating the sand, but the actual seashells have been disappearing faster than cashews out of a bowl of mixed nuts. I am such a people pleaser the thought occurred to me to sneak out after Molly was asleep, buy a few bags of shells, and scatter them around the beach during the night so our shell collecting would be more exciting the next day.

Just then, in the distance, I saw it: a complete shell. Not a fragment, but an untouched, sparkling beauty. I raced toward it to snatch it up before anyone else spotted it. It was my shell and I saw it first. I pulled it from the sand and stared at it intently. I ran my fingers over its smooth surface and thought, *Am I able to pass this piece of Frisbee off to my daughter as a shell?* Previously, I'd tried to pass string beans off to her as Martian spaghetti and that was a no-go, but what the heck, it was worth a try.

I turned around and Molly wasn't there. I turned the other way and scoured the beach. All I could see were adults ignoring the dangers of skin cancer. I'd concentrated so hard on trying to find a seashell for my daughter's enjoyment, I'd neglected to keep track of her whereabouts.

Horrible thoughts flooded my brain. She could swim but was no match for an angry ocean. What if someone had snatched my baby? The news was full of tales of the demented. I tried to keep calm, but couldn't. A panicked tone entered my voice.

"Molly, Molly," I shouted. Nobody answered. Tears began to form. What would I do without her? What would my life be like? How could I exist without my Molly being a part of the world? How could I wake up every morning and not see her sleeping with her three bunnies? I called out one more time.

"Molly. Please, Molly, where are you?"

I heard a giggle.

"Mommy, I'm here. I'm hiding behind you. Every time you turn around, I turn around too so you can't see me."

I scooped her up in my arms and hugged her a little too tightly.

"Mommy, why are you crying?"

"Because, for a minute, I didn't know where you were and I was scared."

"Really scared?" she asked brightly.

"Yes, really scared," I replied.

"Really, really scared?"

"Yes, really, really, *really* scared."

"Mommy, are those real tears?"

"Yes, baby."

"Let's do it again . . . and Mommy?"

"Yes, sweetie?"

"Why are you holding a piece of Frisbee?"

My mother was the worst cook ever. In school, when we traded lunches, I had to throw in an article of clothing.

OH, MOTHER!

It's my contention that the things you remember about your childhood govern the way you raise your own children. Even though my mother died when I was thirteen, I find myself constantly remembering the little things she did for me as I spend time with my daughter.

Kindness was my mother's finest attribute; cooking was her downfall. Luckily, I was not a picky eater. Most of the things she cooked for me I found delicious.

I don't know why my mother resisted the help of recipes. Professional cooks spend a great deal of time perfecting how much of something goes into something else, but my mother preferred to wing it. Her most successful culinary creation (and my all-time favorite) was spaghetti and ketchup mixed with a semi-melted lump of butter. My second favorite was what I called Campbelled rice. This paired instant rice with

27

Campbell's Vegetarian Vegetable soup. Not only was it delicious, it was also educational (if not entirely sanitary), as I would spell out different words on the kitchen table with the gummy letters. If there was any Campbelled rice left the next day, the mixture would be poured into tomato soup, thus creating yet another unique variation: Campbelled tomato rice paste. It was midway between soup and Spackle.

My mother's three most spectacular culinary failures involved a can of corn, a duck, and matzo balls. They were not featured in the same concoction but probably would have tasted better if they had been. I don't know what prompted her to put a closed can of Niblets into the searing oven; I just remember the explosion. I was only around five, but I recall that I was in charge of picking bits of corn off the floor while she climbed the ladder and tackled the ceiling.

My father loved chicken matzo ball soup and complained that the matzo balls from our local delicatessen were inferior to the ones he remembered from his Catskills childhood. He recalled matzo balls that were light and fluffy and yet somehow had a heavier consistency. I think it was the phrase "heavier consistency" that was my father's big mistake. One day my mother set out to make the matzo balls from my father's youth from scratch. I watched her blend eggs, matzo meal, water, a little more matzo meal for heavier consistency, and what appeared to be gunpowder and then attempt to discipline the mixture into the traditional round shape. She then dropped the rolled-up balls of mush into the boiling water and watched them morph. After a few minutes she removed the first specimen from the pot with a slotted spoon and scrutinized it carefully. It was now in the shape of a human liver. She placed it on a paper towel and cut it in half. Although the outside was gummy, the inside was runny, so she stuffed in a little more matzo meal.

"I guess they need more cooking," she said. "I'll cut them all in half and put them back in for a while."

It was like eating dried Silly Putty. We were fearful of breaking the garbage disposal, so the leaden bits of dough were finally tossed in the trash, and all three of us had new respect for the local deli.

My father's "I'm bored with chicken and steak" statement led to the diabolical duck. For this dish my mother enlisted the help of a recipe. Unfortunately, it wasn't a recipe for duck.

"A duck is just like a chicken," she reasoned. "I'll use a recipe for roast chicken."

I remember her taking the duck out of the oven and encountering a sea of grease that in my brief life I had never seen emanate from a chicken. It was so slimy that as my mother served it, the poor bird almost slid off the plate.

Not wanting to waste a perfectly good duck, and continuing to make the faulty chicken/duck comparison, the next day she decided to make duck salad. Adding mayonnaise to a mixture does not make a dish less greasy. My mother put the chopped duck, eggs, celery, and mayonnaise in a bowl, mixed it up, and attempted to make me a duck salad sandwich. Even I said no.

Along with my mother's lack of cooking talent, I also remember her remarkable personality. I remember the light in her eyes whenever she saw me. I remember her kind voice and her forgiving, patient nature. I remember the way she went out of her way to do things to make her little girl happy. I remember the smocking she painstakingly sewed on my pink-striped party dress and her hand-stitching together my first tutu (without a pattern, of course). I remember her surprising me and showing up on parents' day at my summer camp in North Carolina days after undergoing a major operation. I remember her trying her best to keep a smile on her face as she battled a rampant cancer that refused to be abated. Most of all, I remember that she loved me. I still miss her. After all, she only died forty years ago.

Cooking aside, I only hope I'm half as good a mother to my daughter as my mother was to me.

I love to shop. I rationalize shop. I buy a dress because I need change for gum.

GO AHEAD, OPEN
THIS BAG

My father's annual visit always reminded me that as we age we do not become less strange.

This particular year, my father looked a little drained as he shuffled off the plane. His usually neatly positioned white hair was disheveled and his shoulders appeared hunched.

"Dad, good to see you," I exclaimed, administering the two-second father-daughter hug that we had perfected through the years.

"I thought I could do it. Turned out I was mistaken," he whispered dejectedly.

"What do you mean?"

"The bag of peanuts won," my father mumbled.

"You've come all the way from Miami to Las Vegas to visit me. I'm afraid I'm going to have to insist you make sense," I demanded. "What game were you playing with a bag of peanuts?"

"I attacked the bag from every possible angle from the minute the flight attendant handed it to me. I just couldn't open it."

"You spent five and a half hours trying to open a bag of peanuts?"

"No. I rested periodically."

"Didn't the bag have a perforation on one side? Usually, if you look carefully, on one side there's a perforation."

"I checked. There was no perforation. Possibly it was a defective bag. I don't know, I didn't check other people's."

"Why didn't you ask for help?"

"I'm a seventy-eight-year-old, two-hundred-pound man. What do you want me to say to the thirty-year-old, one-hundred-and-fifteen-pound female flight attendant? 'Will you open this bag of peanuts for me?' Why don't I just put on a dress and be done with it?"

"How about the person sitting next to you?"

"I wish you hadn't asked. She was an eighty-year-old ninety-pounder."

"And she opened the bag with no problem?"

"She struggled. She finally stabbed it with a fork over Denver."

"Why didn't *you* stab it once you saw

there was a way in?"

"Because I shouldn't have to. I've raised a daughter, I've been a lawyer. Last year, when the last full-service island closed downtown, I even learned how to pump my own gas. I should be able to open a bag of nuts."

"So what did you eat on the plane?"

My father looked at me in amazement.

"Honey, have you not been listening? I had no time to eat. This was a full-time job."

We had arrived at the car, and I noticed my father reach for the door handle twice before he actually made contact.

"And what did you have to drink?"

"Three martinis."

"Three martinis? Why did you have three martinis?"

"I never gave up hope. I kept thinking I could unlock the secret to the bag, and if I ordered one more martini, I could have the peanuts I deserved with my alcoholic beverage."

"But it never happened and you just tugged at the bag and drank? You didn't tell anyone you were my father, did you?"

"I had no time. Especially after the flight attendant passed out the bag of pretzels."

"Again no perforation?"

"No perforation, but I eventually found a

weaker side and opened the pretzels."

"Thank the Lord."

"Unfortunately, I don't like pretzels. I think they're nothing but burnt bits of bread. I don't understand why people eat them. I think they're more suited for packing material than for munching. It just encouraged me. It gave me a false sense of my own strength and ability and I went back to my original mission."

"Where are the peanuts now?"

"I don't really know."

"What do you mean, you don't know? What did you do with them?"

"Ifflusshdem," he mumbled.

"What?"

"I flushed them."

"You flushed the peanuts down the airplane toilet?"

"Not immediately."

"You didn't," I barked, picturing my seventy-eight-year-old father urinating on a bag of peanuts.

"Yes, I did," my father replied, leaning his head back against the car seat and smiling contentedly. "It was what they deserved."

FUTURE REALITY
SHOWS

WHO WANTS TO EAT A COW DUNG SANDWICH?

Lucky contestants have to eat a cow dung sandwich. We see the actual cows creating the contents of the sandwiches and watch the sandwiches being made. Who can eat it the fastest? The winner gets a million dollars.

WHO WILL SHOOT MY MOTHER?

You explain on national television why you hate her, and the lucky winner gets to have someone shoot her. You choose where and how. You win a million dollars.

WHO WANTS TO MARRY A SERIAL KILLER?

Serial killers fall in love too. Six lucky women get to spend time with a hardened criminal on death row . . . but only one of them gets to marry him, have sex with him, and be present for the execution. You win a million dollars.

WHO WANTS TO BE A SHMILLIONAIRE?

This is just a logical monetary progression of the actual game show. You win a shmillion dollars.

WHO WANTS TO SMASH THEIR HIGH-DEFINITION FLAT-SCREEN TELEVISION SET?

I do. Keep your million dollars.

A HOLE IN EIGHT

When I was in my twenties and a dancer on Broadway, the thought of me holding a golf club was as likely as Eleanor Roosevelt wearing a bikini. To me, golf wasn't even a sport; it was an excuse for older people to wear loud clothing. However, after straining a deltoid muscle playing tennis, tearing an Achilles tendon jogging, and dislocating a disc in my back performing a grande jeté, the concept of golf began to make sense to me.

In our middle age, my husband (whom I shall refer to as Martin because that is his name) and I have spent many a pleasantly frustrating afternoon whacking a small white ball across unforgiving sod. Golf reveals quite a bit about a person's personality; for instance, I have learned that my husband is a perfectionist and that I am totally out of touch with reality.

Here is a typical verbal exchange:

"Good shot," I say to Martin as I watch his golf ball fly high into the sky, swerve horizontally to the right, and land in a massively wooded area.

"Why do you say that? It's not a good shot. It landed in a forest," he replies.

"It looked good to me. It went forward."

"Well, it was seven different types of crap," he exclaims, not using the word *crap.*

"That's not true. There are so many other things that could have gone wrong. You didn't hit a house, you kept hold of the club right to the end, and, as I've proven many times, it is very possible to miss the ball entirely. You have many things to be grateful for."

It is at this moment I shall impart to you my secret to happiness. It can be summed up in two words: low expectations. If you expect to be excellent at something, you will no doubt be disappointed. If you expect to be terrible, you can thrill yourself by actually being almost competent. You cannot low-expectate about everything, however, otherwise you will never make any money and you will have to live outside. I'm talking about things that don't really matter in the long run, and unless you are or are aspiring to be a professional golfer, golf would certainly fall into that category.

That's why I have a good time playing and Martin is continually frustrated.

As frustrated as he is with himself, it is no match for how frustrated he is with me. A few birthdays ago I made the mistake of buying him golf binoculars. This is a contraption that allows you to see how far you are from your ball's destination. If you line it up with the flag, it will give you the correct yardage. If you mistakenly line it up with the mountain behind the flag, it will cause you to swear uncontrollably, choose the wrong club, and ask if you can hit the shot again because it wasn't your fault, it was those damn golf binoculars that your wife bought for you.

I am unable to line up these binoculars correctly, so I am not allowed to touch them.

"How far away from the hole am I?" I asked Martin, estimating myself to be maybe one hundred yards at the most.

Martin picked up the binoculars, squinted, and thought for a second.

"Twenty minutes," he replied.

This was cruel but funny and also correct.

I play with pink balls. This habit immediately warns the poor, unsuspecting people who get paired with me to expect more than a few appalling shots. They are also pleasantly surprised when I land a ball on the fairway. I've heard many players whisper, "We're going to be all right. She's not as bad as I thought she was going to be."

Here is another secret to my golf happiness. The equipment I play with is usually on sale at Target. It seems very few people want to be seen with pink balls. My husband plays with the expensive, super-duper balls that are surgically wrapped around a titanium core and are scientifically proven to go farther and faster, thereby making him apoplectic when he hits them in the water.

Never practice before starting a round. My husband spends at least half an hour practicing his drive, his second shot, his pitch, his chip, his sand shot, and his putt before he tees off, thereby increasing his anger at himself when he is on the course.

"I practiced that shot at the driving range and it was perfect," I hear him moan constantly.

Well, more fool he. If I hit a good shot, I'm thrilled, and if I don't . . . well, what do I care? It's not like I practiced.

The maximum amount of strokes I can take on any given hole is eight. Martin actually instituted this rule in an effort to allow us to finish a round before dark. As a result,

I no longer have to play the par fives. I just sit in the cart and write down an eight. I don't inconvenience other players and I rest up for the next hole.

I don't ever compare myself to the professionals. I figure they can't tell jokes, I can't hit a ball three hundred yards — we're even.

What other nuggets of golfing wisdom can I impart? Don't drink and drive. "I just need to loosen up a little bit" is something I've heard from a variety of men. Very often I'll see a male foursome drinking beer and then trying to hit a ball. As far as I know, there is no scientific proof that alcohol improves aim.

Enjoy just being outside. I always say to myself, "I might have lost a ball, but I've seen a bunny." It's a privilege just to be able to look at a mountain while other people are working in an office.

If nobody sees you take a shot in the sand where the ball moves two inches, forget about it. Many politicians have forgotten things of far greater importance and gotten away with them. Eventually you will achieve a "good out," as they call it. Just count that one.

Sometimes you will be paired with the most annoying people on earth. Put a cell phone to your ear and announce you have to leave because of a family emergency. This always works. Many people have done this to stop playing with me.

Never take a lesson. Just position yourself next to someone who is taking a lesson. This way, if you become worse, you can forget what you overheard, and if you become better, you have had free instruction.

Always aim for the gardener to ensure you won't hit him.

When a new miracle club is advertised on television, don't buy it. It will work, but only the first two times you swing it. It will never work again and you will always be trying to re-create your first two swings.

Try not to become too frustrated when playing behind slow players. Very old people sometimes get together to play golf. In fact, when I first heard the little boy in the movie say, "I see dead people," I thought he was envisioning being behind a senior foursome. Bring along a pack of cards and play a hand if the course gets backed up.

Always keep the cart on the path or on the fairway. Do not attempt to bypass players. You do not — I repeat, *Do not* — know what is waiting for you over the hill. Once my husband became impatient with a foursome in front of us who not only were terrible but were attempting to play from the bionic tees. It was a new cart and the brakes were good, but they were no match for gravity. We ended up asking two young brave boys who worked in the golf shop to haul our formerly new cart out of a lake. It still beeps intermittently, reminding us of what we put it through, and Martin's wallet still smells of fish.

In conclusion, enjoy the good shots and forget the bad; it doesn't matter. I may be out of touch with reality, but I'm having a good time.

I bought a new wrinkle cream. If you use it once a day, you look younger in a month. Twice a day, you look younger in two weeks. I ate it.

AT WHAT PRICE?

How far should people go to achieve fame, and more important, why do they want it? In the past few years we've seen Nick and Jessica ruin their marriage, Whitney and Bobby proudly peddle their dysfunctional relationship, and Anna Nicole film her day-to-day diary of madness that climaxed in her expiring from an overdose.

The habit of exposing intimate details of a life to garner attention has become rampant in our culture. If there is one thought I will drum into my daughter, it is that fame for fame's sake is a completely empty experience. Fame should be a by-product (and not necessarily a good one) of achieving something extraordinary. It can then sometimes, if you're very lucky, become a useful tool to help you achieve something even more extraordinary.

Paris Hilton would not be nearly as popular a figure if her explicit sex video had not flooded the Internet. I'm not saying she released the footage on purpose, but I do think if she had to do it all over again she would have smiled more. Am I wrong in thinking that a sizable portion of the new generation of celebrities can't do anything? Madonna was my generation's Paris Hilton, but at least she could almost sing.

Speaking of Madonna, remember the release of her book that consisted of nothing but naked pictures of herself? Remember the attention that it drew at the time? It all seems rather mild now. Madonna was the bad girl of the late twentieth century and even she has to be saying, "Could these young girls at least stay sober long enough to put on underwear?"

I have a friend who has recently become immensely famous because he is an excellent actor in a very good television show. He is no longer able to open the curtains to his bedroom because of telescopic camera lenses aimed through his windows that can photograph him at any time. His personal life is public speculation in the tabloids, and the majority of the information contained therein is incorrect. A modest amount of media attention is undeniably fun, but as Princess Diana discovered, when you can't turn it off, it can turn deadly.

Let's talk about the camera phone. Not only is it unnecessary, I've never seen a picture of myself on a camera phone where I didn't resemble a German shepherd. Web sites that show photos of celebrities in compromising situations and, even worse, coming home from the dentist are the newspapers of today. These sites are so ubiquitous that the gossipers themselves are now fodder for gossip. They have gossiped so well they are now famous.

Andy Warhol once said, "In the future, everyone will be famous for fifteen minutes." Rita says, "Make that ten." Becoming a television star is now no longer limited to people who have honed their craft and studied for years. Television stars now include people who can stand on a post for hours while holding a dead fish in their mouth.

Even vanity takes a backseat to the opportunity to be on television. Footage of both women and men undergoing plastic surgery proliferates on cable. I cannot remember an evening when I've flipped through channels and haven't seen at least one comatose person having their skin severed with a scalpel by a shower-capped, white-toothed, fame-seeking surgeon. I understand that many of the patients on

49

these shows receive their enhancements for free, but I still think the results might be better had the surgeon not been concerned with operating while showing his good side.

Here's the crux of the problem. It's a noisy culture. The people who are prepared to shout get heard, even if they don't have much to say. The horrific Virginia Tech murders were carried out by a deranged, disenfranchised psychopath who mailed pictures of himself to the media in an effort to be noticed. Osama bin Laden seems to release his videotapes when he feels he's not being sufficiently talked about. Suicide bombers expect to be posthumously revered. I guess this warped quest to be noticed has always been part of the human condition. After all, John Wilkes Booth shot Abraham Lincoln almost 150 years ago . . . but at least John Wilkes Booth was wearing underwear.

Working hard and achieving something isn't easy, but it's what self-respect is all about. To misquote Franklin D. Roosevelt, "The only thing we have to fear is fame for fame's sake."

I had the worst birthday party ever when I was a kid. My parents hired a pony to give rides. And these ponies are never in good shape. This one dropped dead. It just wasn't much fun after that. One kid would sit on him, and the rest of us would drag him around in a circle.

CNNNMSNBC CNBCFOXNEWS NETWORK HEADLINE NEWSLOCALAND NATIONALNEWS

There are too many news outlets and not enough news to go around. I force my eyelids open each morning, search for the remote control in the bed, flick on one of the pastel morning shows, and hear the top stories of the day read to me by a perky but not too perky woman who is not too young and yet not too old. If I go newsless for the next ten hours and invite one of the three network anchors into my living room at six o'clock that evening, I'm more often than not given the same news I listened to for five minutes at eight in the morning, except now it's stretched over twenty-two minutes plus commercials. (I've also noticed that the commercials on the evening newscasts are predominately stomach-related. The news is now so upsetting, drug companies have figured out a way to profit from it.)

The networks are obviously at a disadvantage in this age of immediate information. They are in the delicate position of having to create news that is unique to them. Brian Williams has begun to run stories on people in small towns who whittle, and Katie Couric has introduced the dangerous concept of interactive news.

"Send me a story you'd like to see on the news," she purred one night into the filtered lens. "I'd like to hear it."

Well, I wouldn't. Maybe that's just me, but I like my news to be newsworthy. I like for a story to be so important that reporters feel the need to report it. If I sent in a news story, it might go something like this: "Today I tried a recipe I've never tried before. When a recipe states that dough will not stick to the pan even if you don't grease it beforehand, don't believe it."

At least the evening anchors only have to recite the news once a day. The anchors I feel most sympathy for are the teams on Headline News. Repeating the exact same stories over and over and trying to keep them sounding as if it is the first time they're being read has to be harder than Madonna trying to pretend to be a virgin.

It would be unfair not to note that the fifteen-minute summary of events from around the world is very handy for those of us exercising on a treadmill. I, however, walk for twenty minutes, so I still have to endure five minutes of repetition. The additional information located at the bottom of the screen helps a tad. If I've already heard the disaster du jour, I can always catch up on vital information like last night's scores from the WNBA or the temperature in Anchorage. Other, similar networks employ crawls on the bottom of the screen, which as a rule I attempt to avoid. My eyes tire of the side-to-side motion and I worry that they may wander back and forth involuntarily during the course of a day, causing me to appear shifty.

I am in my best shape during a celebrity murder trial. I can extend my twenty minutes of treadmill to an hour with the aid of an interesting cross-examination. Recently, judges have been ruling against cameras being permitted in the courtroom . . . something about a circus-like atmosphere, using people's misfortune for entertainment, judicial interference, blah blah blah. Do they not care about the state of my inner thighs? Have they no conception of the benefits to my buttocks? If I sent pictures of me before the O. J. trial and then after, they might reconsider.

Another question I have concerns the female news anchors on Headline News. Why are they all beginning to look like models? Where are they finding newswomen these days? *Playboy*? I have nothing against beautiful women getting jobs, but shouldn't the networks at least throw a few hours of broadcasting, if only in the middle of the night, to a woman with a high forehead and a big nose?

The more attractive a woman reporter is on CNN, the more time she gets to spend indoors. If you're over forty and have a double chin, chances are you're filming your report wearing a parka and freezing on the White House lawn or wearing a flak jacket down in a spider hole in Iraq. If you're over fifty and still in front of the cameras, you'd better be blonder than angel food cake and thinner than angel hair pasta. I love Judy Woodruff and Lesley Stahl, but I think the last time they ate something the Beatles were on Ed Sullivan.

"Breaking News" is a graphic that is currently being greatly overused on television to command our attention. The last time I saw it flashed on my TV screen it turned out that someone in a kitchen in Iowa had broken something. My suggestion to keep news fresh is radical but just might be entertaining. Instead of a "Breaking News" graphic, how about a "Made-Up News" graphic? It would keep the Headline News anchors from excruciating repetition and give networks stories that nobody else has.

"Hi, this is Katherine McKennedy and here are today's headlines . . . Tony Danza announces he is running for president of the United States . . . Bill Gates goes bankrupt . . . and Osama bin Laden marries Jennifer Lopez in a drive-through chapel in Vegas. More after these messages."

I don't know about you, but I'm staying tuned.

I'm an only child, which means I was very overprotected. My tricycle had seven wheels. And a driver.

AND AWAY IT WENT

In an effort to take a mental vacation from everyday annoyances, Martin and I decided we wanted a hobby. Did we choose something sensible, like stamp collecting? Or maybe something tranquil, like canasta? Was it something fun, like wine tasting? Oh, no. We decided to take up the greatest cash-losing hobby of all time . . . horse racing.

It wasn't as arbitrary as it sounds. Martin's father had worked in racing in England, so Martin had practically grown up on racecourses. It would be a thrill not only for him but for his parents to be actually standing in the winner's circle alongside a victorious horse instead of standing on the sidelines.

We had no idea how to go about buying a racehorse. I was no help. I suggested a used-horse lot but couldn't find any listings in the yellow pages. One day Martin arrived at home with a horse racing magazine. He'd had an idea. We didn't really want to spend a great deal of money on something that risky, so instead of buying all of a cheap racehorse, why not buy part of an expensive one? There was an ad in the back of *Horsing Around* that listed the number for a horse syndicate contact. Martin wasted no time in setting up a meeting.

I grew a little suspicious when we were told to meet our contact in a parking lot behind a drugstore.

"Rita, I grew up on racecourses. These guys are all a little shifty. This is the way they operate."

On a crisp Sunday morning we parked our car behind Rite-Aid and watched for a cranberry Camaro. Five minutes later it appeared and parked next to us. A wiry man in his fifties exited the car. He was wearing a lint-covered navy blue blazer and an insincere smile. He extended his hand.

"Hi, Marty, Rita. I'm Benny. Nice to meet ya."

We had our horse meeting in the front seat of his car. Benny had an overseas connection and together he and the connection were importing racehorses to America from New Zealand. For some reason, certain New Zealand horses could enter less competitive races in the United States than they could at home. The system was complicated but legal. Benny showed us photos of a beautiful horse waiting to be transported.

"This horse is a proven winner. I have three investors, and I just need one more to finalize the sale."

Martin and I discussed the pros and cons of the situation and decided that this would be the cheapest way to get horse racing out of our system. We would write the check, have some fun, and lose some money. End of hobby.

I forget the actual name of the horse, so I'll call her Anorexic Annie. Annie was not a good traveler. She arrived in America dehydrated and jet-lagged. The flight from New Zealand to Los Angeles is fifteen hours long; I'd have hated to be the person sitting next to her.

Martin and I visited Annie regularly and brought her carrots and flowers. She ate both. When she was finally well enough to race, I have to admit it was exciting. Martin and I went backstage to where the horses prepare and visited Annie in her dressing stable. We watched her walk around the ring and compared her against her competition. She was looking good.

The race was over in a matter of minutes, and the results were the worst of both worlds. Annie hadn't won or lost. She had come in third in a close race. Not only had she come in third, she had incurred a slight injury. A small crack had appeared in her left front hoof.

We couldn't give up on Annie because she had potential. She had only been beaten by a length and a half. All we had to do was heal a small crack in her hoof. How hard could that be? We found out when the medical bills began to arrive. I was never present when the acupuncture was administered, but I can only imagine the needles being stuck into Annie's hoof as she was asked, "Do you feel this? How about this?" We also received bills for massage and hydrotherapy. I was expecting one for psychiatry, but luckily it never arrived.

Annie was never fit enough to race again, but we had won a little bit of money (not enough to cover our investment) and had some fun. Soon Benny had another horse ready to get on the plane. This one was even better.

We went to the airport to greet Bipolar Barry as he exited the plane. He was a big boy and he was beautiful. He was a striking shade of chestnut with a white marking down the front of his long nose that to me looked like a dollar sign. Bipolar Barry arrived in better physical shape than Anorexic Annie but seemed lethargic. After a few days our trainer made the diagnosis that he was depressed. He missed his friends and his hay. He needed to get out and meet other horses. Yes, a horse psychiatry bill was in our future.

Bi-Po eventually got into a better mood, and the first race he was entered in, he won! We were all there and got our picture taken in the winner's circle. My husband's parents were present, and they couldn't have been more chuffed (the English word for "proud"). We had done it. We had defied the odds and had purchased a part of a prizewinning racehorse for a bargain price. I had visions of being interviewed at the Kentucky Derby.

"Did you ever think your horse would win the Derby?" the announcer would ask me.

"I had a feeling he was a winner, but really I owe everything to his psychiatrist," I would answer.

That evening Martin and I had a discussion about buying out our other racehorse partners. We were cut short by a phone call the next morning.

"Hi, Marty, Rita. Benny here. I want you both on the line for this. I have some bad news."

"What happened?" I asked. "He didn't really win? It was a hologram?"

"Is he injured? Can we make him better? Does he need a vacation?" Martin asked.

"He dropped dead."

"What?" we both screamed into our phone receivers.

"The trainer was walking him in a circle this morning and it appears he had a massive heart attack."

"Oh, thank God," I said. "It was the trainer who dropped dead. I thought it was the horse."

"It *was* the horse," Benny stated. "We won't know officially if it was a heart attack until the autopsy."

There it was, the final bill for Bipolar Barry — a horsetopsy. The horsetopsy concluded that Barry had had an enlarged heart. I was glad we hadn't found out about the enlarged heart while he was still alive because I'm sure Benny would have found a veterinarian who performed horse heart transplants. That would have been a bill to remember.

Our horse adventure continued because now we had been in the winner's circle and we were not going to stop. Like the lottery winner who hits a jackpot and keeps buying tickets, we wanted to experience the rush again, and Benny had a healthy, well-adjusted, normal-hearted horse already on a plane.

Fickle Frank was a winner. The first time he raced he came in second. Then third, then, yes, first. We stood in the winner's circle once again. We were sick when the trainer told us about his tongue.

"He can't control it when he races. It's too long and we have to strap it down. It's not going to be long before he's going to bite it and then he's through. I have a buyer and I think we should sell him while we can still get a good price."

It was a tough decision, but this would officially put us in the black. I can't remember, but I think we made about $3,000 on Fickle Frank. It pales in comparison when we found out that Frank had gone on to win many races after the sale. Evidently his new owners had his tongue under control. We stopped paying attention when Frank passed the half-million-dollar mark in winnings. We had finally bought a prize race-horse that couldn't stop winning, and we no longer owned it.

I don't know if Benny is still in business, but we finally stopped accepting his calls. I'm sure he has another horse ready to board a plane, but we officially ended that hobby and began a new one — golf. It's expensive and frustrating, but at least we know that our clubs will never need acupuncture, hydrotherapy, or autopsies. There is, however, a possibility that if we don't eventually improve, Martin and I will soon need psychiatrists.

I had the most boring office job in the world. I used to clean the windows on the envelopes.

AND THE GIFT BASKET GOES TO . . .

"A gift basket will be arriving at your home in approximately half an hour," the voice on the other end of the phone stated. "Will someone be there to accept it?"

I looked over at my hungry husband, who was ready to overpay for food at our local restaurant just to be fed.

"Can you leave it at the front door?"

"No, there must be someone there to accept it."

"OK, we'll wait."

When I got off the phone, my husband asked, "Wait for what? I'm hungry."

"We have to wait for the Oscar gift basket."

"I'm waiting for a gift basket? I'm waiting for old apples in a straw box to be delivered to my door? I don't think so."

"It's only five o'clock. The restaurant doesn't even open until five-thirty. It'll be here in less than half an hour. Sit down and have a cracker."

Thirty minutes in, just when Martin was about to tie me up and throw me into the car, the doorbell rang.

"Oscar gift basket."

I buzzed it in. I was not ready for what arrived.

It was 2001, and it was the first time I had been asked to write jokes for the Oscars. The whole experience was already overwhelming. I was in a room with Steve Martin and three other writers and we were fashioning Steve's monologue bit by bit. I had never written jokes for anyone but me, so the experience was more than a little daunting, but not nearly as daunting as the large, dead body covered in a horse blanket being wheeled into our foyer.

"What *is* this?" I screeched.

"It's the Oscar gift basket. It's worth thousands of dollars and weighs sixty pounds," the deliveryman explained, hinting for a tip.

I gave him twenty dollars. He seemed a little too happy and left. But what did I care? I had the Oscar gift basket.

Suddenly Martin wasn't so hungry. We removed the horse blanket and stared at what lay beneath.

"I'll get the scissors," he said.

Let me just state that when I agreed to write for the Oscars, I knew nothing about the basket. I was just honored to have been asked. I didn't even inquire about the money (scale). I simply wanted the experience. Sometimes things actually surprise you in a good way.

Here is a partial list of what we received. It is a few years later, so I'm sure I'll leave something out, but don't worry. You'll still be impressed.

1. A Christian Dior handbag. Brown and beautiful. I was very happy.
2. A digital camera. Small and silver. My husband was very happy.
3. A certificate for a two-day stay in a suite at the Ritz-Carlton of our choice. We were both very happy.
4. A certificate for a two-week safari in Africa. We were both a little afraid.
5. Crystal candlesticks.
6. A fantastic Fendi silver watch for a female.
7. A fantastic Fendi silver watch for a male.
8. Bottles of vodka, champagne, and cognac.
9. His-and-hers designer sunglasses. (I

can't remember the designer and we lost the glasses some time ago.)

10. A huge box of Godiva chocolates.
11. A fringed silk scarf.
12. A certificate for the use of the newest model of BMW for two weeks.
13. A certificate for a new bed that conforms to your body.
14. A bottle of Joy perfume.
15. Multiple bottles of glorious creams and lotions.
16. A $200 gift card for Lancôme makeup.
17. A $250 gift card for Banana Republic.
18. A $250 gift card for Old Navy.
19. A leather wallet.
20. A certificate for a new office chair.
21. United Airlines flight upgrades.
22. Magic pimple cream.
23. A certificate for a free shot of Botox.
24. A free facial and body massage at a glamorous spa.
25. A silver picture frame.
26. And finally, certificates for a teeth-whitening session and LASIK eye surgery.

Now, I'm sure I'm leaving things out, but I'm also sure you're impressed. I certainly was. It was Christmas in October. The next year I was fortunate to be asked to write for the Oscars again. I was flattered, but before officially accepting I said, "Yes, on the condition I get the basket."

My last credit card bill was so big, before I opened it I actually heard a drumroll.

And Up

Reading a fashion magazine the other day, I discovered an article entitled "How to Look Good in Your Twenties, Thirties, Forties, and up."

It was bad enough that the fifties were not included as a decade, but the word *up* wasn't even capitalized. It was as if the editors of the magazine felt it best not to draw attention to the fact that an "and up" person might read the magazine, in case it adversely affected their advertising revenue.

I am "and up." So are many of my friends. One of them recounted to me a phone call she had gotten recently. It was an unsolicited telemarketing call, and because she was brought up to be a wee bit too polite, instead of slamming down the receiver she decided to answer the ensuing questions to the best of her ability.

The phone rings. My friend answers it.

73

My friend: Hello?

Unsolicited caller: Hello, could I take a few minutes of your time to answer some questions?

M.F.: Sure.

U.C.: Are you in the eighteen-to-twenty-nine age group?

M.F.: No.

U.C.: Are you in the twenty-nine-to-thirty-nine age group?

M.F.: No.

U.C.: Are you in the thirty-nine-to-forty-nine age group?

M.F.: No.

U.C.: (Hangs up.)

My friend never got the chance to find out which product was being researched because, being over fifty, she was deemed irrelevant. She began the conversation thinking she was doing the telemarketer a favor and ended up being insulted and having to resort to a midmorning gin and tonic.

The logic of ignoring baby boomers escapes me. We make up 27.5 percent of the population; our average annual household pretax income is $57,700, and collectively our annual spending power is $2.1 trillion a year. Why do they hate us?

The reasoning I've heard is that after age

fifty, people's brand loyalties are deemed to be set in cement. There is assumed to be nothing a commercial or print advertisement can entice us with that will make us open our wallets to a new product.

I'm sorry, but my experience says otherwise. More often than not, I am so dissatisfied with the current brand of whatever I am using that I can't wait to be lied to and sold something promising to be better. My family has owned four different brands of computers and I can guarantee you that a fifth is in our future. I am also a bargain seeker. I love an open-box special or a rebate coupon that is so difficult to fill out that I give up halfway through and pretend it never existed. I also respond to pretty colors; package something in a bright pink box and chances are I'll buy it. I'm not proud of these characteristics, but I'm being honest so as to make my point.

Now, I know there are a few twentysomethings out there who are billionaires. They invented a dot-com company and sold it before anyone realized it was nonsense. Or their parents toiled so hard they died at an early age and left behind a fortune for their offspring. Them apart, I remember how much money I had in my twenties: I could just about afford my rent and bus fare. Why are advertisers so keen to sell things to people who are barely keeping their gelled heads above water? The twentysomethings I know are still being at least partially supported by their fiftysomething parents.

I rarely see someone over thirty in a car commercial. Rationally, how is someone in the eighteen-to-twenty-nine age group going to be able to afford a new automobile? Where did they make $30,000? At the gym? Unless they're selling drugs, chances are they're going to have to smile prettily at Mommy and Daddy for financial aid. Wouldn't advertisers be better served by car commercials aimed at the people who are actually going to fork over the money for the car?

"You've had a baby. You've raised it to the best of your ability. You've paid for the finest education you could afford. Now you've let your baby loose in this crazy world where people drive like maniacs, and all you can do is hope for the best. You built the child, we built the car that will keep that child alive. The Toyota Bodyguard: the only car on the road that comes with a driver." I'd buy one for my daughter now and she's five.

As far as other products go, write "low fat" on it and I'll try it. Make it smell like daisies in a field and I'm there . . . even though I have no idea what daisies in a field smell like. The only products that are being directly marketed to my age group and above are prescription medications. If I had osteoporosis or had to go to the bathroom forty times a day, I'd feel included. The problem is I don't have either of these ailments just yet, although I am thinking of signing up for the medications so they'll keep the advertisements on the air. It's the only time I see an actress over fifty on television.

Contrary to Madison Avenue's beliefs, I feel that in our fifties we are more likely to try new things and have more money to try them. We're living longer, and not only that, we're keeping our teeth. As Glenn Close said in whatever that movie was called (OK, I'll admit my memory isn't what it used to be), "I will not be ignored."

And just so you know how prevalent the baby boomers remain, while you were reading this article, three more people turned fifty. Their husbands and wives and friends threw them big birthday parties and bought them lots of expensive presents. Take that, you telemarketers.

I can never ask for money back after I've loaned it to a friend and they forget to return it. The most I can do, when I'm over their house, is break something of that approximate value.

CASUALTIES

It seems that with every passing year people's dress habits become more and more casual. The "I'm on my way to the gym" look has gradually taken over the world. I think sneakers have to accept some of the blame. The casual look definitely began with feet. Once you have casual feet, why not continue up? I will go out on a limb here and say that 99 percent of the people who wear jogging suits have never jogged and will never do so. I know; I'm one of them.

My husband and I were dropping my daughter off at school the other morning. "Why do all the mothers look like they're in the Olympics?" Martin asked.

"Sweatpants are not only for people who sweat," I replied. "They're also for people who have to get their child to school so early that they can't work a button or a zipper. And there's a plus: if they ever get the urge to do any exercise, they're ready."

Mothers getting their children to school on time are not the only clothing offenders. I was flying cross-country a few weeks ago and a man walked onto the plane wearing something he must have purchased from a shop called Hawaiian Nightmare. There should be a law limiting how many colors are permitted to appear on one shirt, and this man should have been arrested. His look was completed with baggy shorts, a backward baseball cap, and flip-flops. I'm not saying it's wrong to be comfortable on a long trip, but a plane is not a beach. I felt like adding sand to the floor so he could build a castle. The man's hair appeared to have been cut by a weed whacker, and his two-day stubble contained bits of food. I wouldn't have minded so much if he hadn't been the pilot.

Ok, I'm kidding, but it was the attire of the man sitting next to me and it was a good joke.

As with anything, moderation is the key. My in-laws are on the opposite side of the clothing coin. When traveling on a twelve-hour flight from England to Las Vegas, my father-in-law dons a suit and tie and my mother-in-law will not enter an airport unless she's wearing high heels, stockings, and a girdle. Oh yes, and a dress. I don't want to get her arrested. Wait, maybe I do. Anyway, when we greet them in Las Vegas, due to lack of circulation they are usually a light shade of blue.

The embellished jean was "jeanius." I don't know who thought of adding sequins and rhinestones to farm attire, but it works for me. It says, *Yes, I'm casual, but I'm also dressed up and ready to party.* I'll pay six times more for a pair of jeans that sport Swarovski crystals than I will for a pair that has pockets. I don't know who this guy Swarovski is, but he's everywhere. He's on my handbags, in my hair, and around my neck. The two men I now spend the most time with are my husband and Swarovski.

Now, as I've told you, I love jeans, but the low, tight jean is a fashion that only 2 percent of the women in America can wear attractively. Unfortunately, it is being worn by at least 62 percent. I can't help thinking that if these women can afford the latest fashion statement, they can also afford a mirror. My husband and I were walking along the street the other day and passed an ample woman wearing tight, low-cut jeans and a short knit cropped top. Her middle bulged generously. My husband looked at her and uttered, "That reminds me . . . I have to check my tires."

My daughter wears a school uniform. Yes, the children look a little Stepfordy, but they do look neat. I think clothing can influence behavior. My daughter is definitely more polite when she has her blouse tucked in.

The clothing of young boys mystifies me. I'm told the baggy look originated because it made it easy to conceal weapons and the look just caught on with the male population. At this point not only could they conceal weapons, they could conceal washing machines. They're not even pants anymore; they're socks with a belt. And all these kids are on cell phones. What are they saying? "Hey, dude, how many times did you trip over your pants today?"

If the world continues this clothing downslide, people will soon be getting married in pajamas. We've gone from wearing suits of armor to wearing tablecloths. Comfort is important, but aesthetics count too. If not, let's all cut holes in sheets and stick our heads through them. (However, let's first make sure they're colored or patterned so nobody thinks we're bigots.)

I do feel better when I make even the slightest of efforts to spruce myself up. In fact, I'm going to go change. Today I'm not picking up my daughter from school wearing a jogging suit. I'm not wearing blue jeans with Swarovski crystals. No, I'm wearing a dress, high heels, makeup, earrings, and my good watch. Oh, whom am I kidding? I'm staying in my jogging suit. It's more comfortable, and who knows, I might even get the urge to jog.

I used to be a vegetarian, but I quit because it has side effects. I found myself sitting in my living room, starting to lean toward the sunlight.

CHRISTMAS RAP

There is a downside to being happily married to the same man for eighteen years. Every year the holidays arrive and I have to find something to give my husband that he wants and that I haven't already given him.

Annoyingly, there has never been anything Martin has given me that I haven't absolutely loved. I feel one of my main attributes is my ability to enjoy gifts. Many women who have been married for over fifteen years adopt the "buy it yourself, wrap it yourself, open it Christmas morning, and pretend to be surprised" method of gift giving, but my husband happens to have great taste. I married a straight guy with a queer eye. Sweaters, blouses, dresses, jewelry — he has never gone wrong. Everything he chooses also fits me perfectly. Either he's very smart or he has a girlfriend who is exactly my size.

One evening, attempting to walk off a particularly fattening Italian dinner, we strolled past an upmarket men's store. Martin looked into the store window, then looked down at his jacket and said (and I quote), "I need a new leather jacket. Look at this."

He pointed to the breast pocket, which was drooping, and then to the hip pocket, where the stitching had begun to fray.

"Someday I would love to own a really expensive black leather jacket."

Now, everybody knows that if you say this to your wife at the end of November, then a black leather jacket will duly appear underneath your Christmas tree at the end of December. By the way, I'm Jewish, but I celebrate Christmas too and I'm going to do that until the Jewish people decide on a way to spell Chhhaanukkkaaah.

He continued.

"I need a new pair of black dress shoes too, and a new belt. This one is too big — I'm losing weight."

"Hallelujah."

"What did you say?" my husband asked.

I then realized I was so overcome with joy, I had said it out loud.

"Nothing, I was just clearing some phlegm. Hhhhaaalleah. There, that's better."

I had my three presents. No more combing the shopping malls and ending up with a talking meat thermometer and a toe massager. This would be the Christmas where the shopping would take me almost no time and the presents would become instant classics. I don't have to tell you that when a woman buys clothes, they last a season; when a man buys clothes, they last a lifetime. My grandfather still wears his Cub Scout uniform.

I glowed with the confidence of a television presenter when I returned home from my shopping expedition the following week. The whole trip had taken exactly three hours and I was finished shopping for my husband. I was careful to revisit the men's store we had passed on our calorie-burning stroll the week before. The jacket in the window that he had coveted happened to be his exact size. It was expensive, but what the hell? It would be worth it just to see the Yuletide joy on his face when he slipped his arms into the silk-lined sleeves. I also bought a black belt one size smaller than the one currently hanging in his closet and a pair of black dress shoes that were almost identical to the ones he had been wearing for the past fifteen years. How could I miss? I was so certain that I had hit a holiday home run, I didn't even bother with the little gifts I usually pepper his Christmas mornings with to increase my odds of buying something he likes. No reindeer boxer shorts or Santa golf balls to wrap this year. This year I was only bringing out the big guns.

It was a particularly pleasant Christmas morning because our baby was a year and a half old. The Christmas before, being only six months old, she'd really only joined in when we rolled her around on the used wrapping paper, but this year she was big enough to destroy. We opened the baby's presents first: a dollhouse, clothes, shoes, stuffed animals, and of course that musical toy that rolls around on the floor and not only drives you crazy but eventually can get you evicted. (Thanks, Auntie Joyce.)

Then it was my turn. I opened the small square box that had to be jewelry, and there they were: the pink sapphire earrings I had admired six months ago. He had done it again, but this time so had I.

I decided to start off with the belt. The wrapping was off, the box was opened, and the belt emerged like a newborn from the crinkly tissue paper. He held it up.

"I like it," he said. "Let's see if it fits."

He wrapped it around his waist and began to tug.

"What size is this?" he asked.

"It's one size smaller than the belt you told me was too big."

He tugged some more.

"I'll exchange it tomorrow," I said.

"You can just return it. I like the one I have."

The shoes were next.

"These are very nice, but they're stiff. My old shoes have molded to my feet."

"Put them with the belt."

It was two strikes, and I was down to the final pitch.

"I know you're going to love this," I said hopefully.

He stared at the baby-soft leather jacket cradled in its paper nest. He lifted it out and slipped one arm into a sleeve and then the other. He zipped it up. The sleeves were too long, the jacket was too short, the circumference too tight. He looked like he'd stolen a jacket.

"I know this was very expensive and I appreciate the thought," he said. "But what the hell were you thinking?"

"I didn't think. I didn't have to. We walked past the store and you pointed to it and said, 'I want an expensive leather jacket,' and then you said, 'My belt is too big and I need new shoes.' "

"I was just talking. I have all those things."

"But I was so certain that you said it because that's what you wanted. I pointed to the earrings because I liked them, not for finger exercise."

He gave me a hug.

"And I'm glad you like them."

"It's not fair. I love them."

I removed myself from his sympathizing embrace.

"Well, what did you want?" I asked.

"A rare book."

"A rare book? You don't have any rare books."

"I know. That's why I wanted one."

Men!

The good news is, I found a first-edition Raymond Chandler novel on the Internet and it arrived before Easter. He loved it, even though he'd read it before.

SUPERFICIAL NIGHTMARES OF THE OVERPRIVILEGED WOMAN

I am a tiny bit ashamed to admit this, but lately I've been having superficial nightmares. I've been waking up in a cold sweat over the following:

1. I splurge on a deluxe pedicure and the next morning I wake up to find the polish completely gone.
2. I'm on the phone at the hairdresser's and when I arrive home, I realize that I wasn't paying attention and that he has parted my hair on the wrong side.
3. My daughter refuses to wear pink.
4. Robbers break in to my house and steal my expensive handbag.
5. We're on vacation and find out there is a special deal that includes breakfast and champagne at sunset and everyone was aware of it except us. The general manager is on vaca-

tion and no one has the authority to alter our vacation package.

6. Inexplicably, the diamond ring my husband bought me for our fifteenth anniversary becomes cloudy. There is no remedy.
7. Starbucks no longer makes low-fat lattes.
8. There is no bottled water anywhere.
9. I wake up to find a new building has been erected in front of my apartment window, totally blocking my view.
10. My Jacuzzi is broken. There is no access panel door to be found and the plumber has to chip through the marble to gain access. After the motor is repaired, a match to the marble cannot be found and the entire surround has to be replaced. (This actually happened, and let me tell you, it was a nightmare.)

DINING IN THE DARK

"What's for dinner?" my husband asked.

"It depends on what you want. We can have either Chinese, Italian, or Thai delivered. I'm very versatile," I replied.

"I have an idea. And don't shoot me down — hear me out. Why don't we venture out where the food actually lives, for a change?"

"You mean you want us to go to the food instead of the food coming to us? Are you insane?" I retorted.

"Rita, there are people who eat in restaurants on a regular basis."

"Maybe they're homeless."

"No, these are people who get out of their sweatpants and into clothes that have zippers and order from waiters and waitresses."

"OK. Should we have Chinese, Italian, or Thai?"

"We're going to try something different. We're going to eat in a trendy restaurant aimed at the desirable eighteen-to-thirty-nine-year-old age group," my husband said, reaching for a magazine he had recently purchased featuring "The Top Ten Hottest Places to Eat in L.A."

"What if they don't let us in? I hear they card people over forty now at these places. It will be so humiliating."

"I've already thought of that. I'm bringing a copy of our latest bank statement and a picture of our beach house. I feel we can overcome our age problem with our financial achievements."

"OK. First let me try to get a reservation in Trendyland."

"Call this number and try to sound young."

"Hello — I mean, hi — like, we'd like to book a table, like, for two . . . Like, for tonight at, like, seven . . . Well, when is the first open reservation? . . . Yes, we can come in three weeks, but we're going to be mighty hungry . . . Yes, I'll hold . . . OK, great — I mean, awesome . . . Yes, I realize how lucky we are . . . My name is Rudner . . . No, not Rubner, *Rudner. D* like in *dysentery* . . . Why do you need our phone number? . . . OK, but we're not going to cancel, we know how lucky we are . . . Why do you need our credit card number? Are you going to charge us for the call? . . . OK, but I swear we're not going to cancel . . . Yes, I'm still aware that we're, like, very lucky . . . Thank you very much. We'll see you then."

I hung up the phone.

"We are so lucky. They've had a cancellation for tonight at ten-thirty."

"Ten-thirty? I thought you were pushing it asking for seven. We usually eat at six."

"Well, we can't cancel. They'll have us arrested."

"Great. So we're going out to dinner half an hour after I go to sleep."

"This was your idea. I was happy with vegetable moo shu."

We whipped ourselves into a caffeine frenzy so as to stay awake past our bedtime and at ten o'clock backed our trendily jeaned selves and our car out of our garage and headed toward unfamiliar territory.

"I'm glad we did this. We never go out at night. This is good," Martin insisted, stifling a yawn.

As we pulled up in front of the Japanese/ Somalian restaurant a red-jacketed valet child opened the door for me.

"Welcome to Auravooshi."

Martin handed the valet his car keys. The juvenile advanced our car three feet, got out, and closed the door.

"I could have done that," Martin whispered. "Then I wouldn't have had to give a twelve-year-old the keys to my very nice car."

The young woman who greeted us at the hostess's podium was clad in a black turtleneck minidress and wearing the sort of microphone mouthpiece employed by the likes of Britney Spears and Christina Aguilera.

"Are these singing waitresses?" I whispered to my husband.

"I don't know," he whispered back, spotting a man on the restaurant floor wearing a black suit and apparently speaking into his breast pocket. "To me they look like they're working for the CIA."

"Rudner. Party of two for ten-thirty," I said politely.

The hostess's lacquered red fish lips parted and said, "It'll be a few minutes."

She then turned away and whispered something into her mouthpiece.

Martin turned and whispered into my earpiece.

"She's telling someone we're too old and to sit us in a dark corner. I don't like it here. Let's go."

"I told you, we can't cancel. They'll report us to the police."

"We're not canceling. We showed up, they

didn't have our table ready, and we left. No judge will convict us."

We waited another ten minutes.

"Hold on a second. They have our Master-Card number and our car. Maybe this is just a front and they're out driving around and charging things to our credit card."

Just then a tattooed, multiply pierced, goateed CIA operative approached us.

"Mr. and Mrs. Rubner? We have your table ready now. Follow me."

As we entered the spooky room, my attention was caught by a wall that appeared to be on fire.

"That's interesting," I remarked.

"It's a new projection technique. There are only four reactive projectors in the world and we own two."

"Who owns the other two?" I asked.

"Unfortunately, the restaurant across the street," he replied.

I tripped over a large round object.

"Excuse me," I said to the beanbag chair.

"Would you like to sit in our casual room or our table-dining room?"

"As much as I'd like to eat off the floor, let's try table dining," my husband said.

We felt our way to a long, low leather banquette situated in front of a sparsely set table. We wedged ourselves into the small space between them and then attempted to adjust our backsides on the cow-covered cushions.

"Are you cool? Sometimes people your age need extra pillows for lumbar support."

"We're very cool," I replied, ignoring my spine's plea for help.

"Brish will be your waiter."

"Are you sure this wasn't one of the Ten Most Uncomfortable Restaurants in L.A.?" I asked Martin as our escort disappeared into the darkness.

A shadow appeared over our dimly lit table. In the gloom, I discerned the outline of a looming human figure.

"Hello, my name is Brish. I'll be happy to answer any questions you have about the menu."

"OK, Brish. Here's the first one. Where is it?"

"You're sitting on it."

Evidently, a popular new game being played at restaurants around the country is Find the Menu. Sitting down for lunch with an old friend a few weeks ago, I reached for what I thought was the napkin under my silverware and sneezed into a list of foods available that day.

Neither Martin nor I had brought a flash-light, so were unable to read our menus. I was therefore forced to utter a sentence I'd never imagined I would ever say.

"We're in your hands, Brish."

Brish proceeded to recommend and order his favorite dishes: a raw fish cocktail served in a martini glass, a whole fish cooked in a lampshade, and chocolate antennae for dessert.

When we arrived back at our car, my husband tipped the valet, slid into an electronically repositioned seat, peered into a readjusted mirror, and turned on a rap station he'd never known his radio possessed.

"He drove this car three feet. When did he have the time to @%^$#*& everything up?"

Two hundred and fifty dollars later we were back home and hungry.

"We did it," my husband proclaimed proudly. "We went someplace new and tried something different."

"Yes, we did," I replied. "Let's never do it again."

I'm a little compulsive about my weight. I weigh myself constantly. What I do is I slowly lower myself down onto the scale, while balancing from the shower curtain rod, and when I reach the weight I want to be, I black out.

DRIVE-BY HOOTING

Let me begin by admitting to you that I am not a good driver. I learned the skill late in life, and to this day, before I start the engine I look down at my right foot and tell myself, *The big one is the brake.*

That being said, I feel my driving is magnificent compared to what I see being perpetrated on the roads today.

Maybe I'm simply unaware of this, but let me ask the question anyway: Are they selling cars without signals these days? I can't tell whether the car makers are cheaper or whether people are just being frugal and don't want to use up their signals. Maybe nowadays people are merely unwilling to offer the assurance a signal demands: "I might go left, I might go right. I'm just not ready to make a commitment."

Of course, I have the opposite problem. If I want to turn, I begin signaling three blocks ahead of the actual street in preparation for my eventual turn. I also confess to being one of those annoying drivers who forget to turn the signal off. I find the clicking comforting. It's consistent and has a beat. It's like a radio without the commercials.

Oh, and speaking of music, I'd like to thank all of the considerate people driving on the roads today who are concerned that other people don't have radios in their cars and so play theirs loud enough for everyone to hear. I'm especially appreciative when the bass is so loud that the sound carries into my bedroom while I'm asleep and I dream the world is blowing up.

Why is the speed limit posted on signs along the nation's highways no longer taken seriously? Recently, while I dutifully obeyed the sixty-five-miles-an-hour limit, the driver of the car behind me became increasingly agitated. I double-checked my speedometer and made sure I was traveling at the maximum speed. I ignored the hooting. A siren began to sound. I looked in my rearview mirror and noticed the impatient driver behind me was the Highway Patrol. He was gesturing at me to speed up. I pulled over and he sailed past. He wasn't chasing anyone, either. I guess he just had to get to Starbucks in a hurry.

Everybody is in a hurry. Recently a city

bus with an accordion middle suddenly pulled out in front of me with no warning. It isn't easy for one of these buses to maneuver. They are the manatees of the vehicle family. Admittedly, the driver of the bus did that for a reason. The reason was he was behind a bus and he didn't like it. To me, if you're a bus, you should accept that fact and stay behind a brother bus. It's like my eighty-nine-year-old aunt not wanting to live in a retirement community with the old people. It's a deal that must be done.

I'd also like to point out the fact that honking doesn't make cars disappear. Very often I'm stuck in traffic and suddenly I find myself in the middle of a horn concerto. I know horn honking makes people feel better temporarily, but it achieves so little in the long term. It's not that other drivers have simply forgotten to move forward; the backup is usually caused by orange cones forcing cars into a single lane for no reason. I will say that there's one situation when I actually like having people honk at me, and that's when I'm waiting to make a left turn; that's how I know the coast is clear and it's time to turn.

People are reluctant and indeed belligerent when it comes to admitting they have made a driving mistake. Let's face it, driving is at best a series of near misses. I feel lucky every time I return to my house alive. In my driving life I've been involved in one traffic accident and hundreds of traffic incidents. An accident is a collision where there is either vehicle damage or someone is injured. An incident is when another driver is temporarily inconvenienced and swears at you. When I'm at fault in a traffic incident, I always mouth the words "I'm sorry." Recently a car backed into me while I was exiting a shopping mall. Nobody was hurt and there was only microscopic damage to my front bumper. The driver of the vehicle that backed into me bolted out of his car and screamed, "I didn't see you!"

I just don't know what my response to that accusation should have been. "Wait there, I'll buy a bigger car"? "Can I pay to have your eyes checked"? "It's my fault. There are moments in the day when both I and my car become invisible"? I'm aware that insurance companies tell you not to admit guilt at the scene of the accident, but I don't feel that failing to look in your rearview mirror before you reverse is defensible.

The other day at a red light, the opposite happened. I stopped and the car behind me continued. Luckily, he wasn't traveling at a speed that could cause any damage, but it was a jolt. He jumped out of the car and screamed into my window, "I was on the phone!"

Again, I'm unaware as to what my response should have been. "I'm sorry to have interrupted your call"?

The driving-and-phoning thing has, of course, become so out of hand that it has been banned in many cities, and I'm hoping all other cities will follow that lead. How did splitting your focus while driving a heavy steel vehicle become so popular? For all you busy executives who think you can't live without a car phone, the solution is simple: you need a car assistant, a little person who lives in the trunk and who, when necessary, sits beside you to dial and express your needs to your clients. Of course, that solution has its problems too, since even listening to someone else's conversation is distracting. Whenever I'm on the phone and my husband is driving, he invariably gets lost.

I saw a frightening report on one of the TV magazine shows recently about video screens inside cars. These are designed not for the restless children in the backseat but for the restless adult in the driver's seat. Yes, there are now cars that are equipped with multiple screens that can be tuned to different channels. Evidently, there is currently no law on the books that prevents a person from watching television while driving, presumably because lawmakers didn't have the foresight to predict the level of stupidity some human beings are capable of achieving. Eventually, watching television while driving will be outlawed, and while we're rewriting driving laws, we should add a few extra, just in case:

No sewing while driving.
No bowling while driving.
No barbecuing while driving.
No washing your hair while driving.
No cutting your toenails while driving.
No welding while driving.
No glassblowing while driving.
No performing circumcisions while driving.

I think this essay is finished. So I'm going to put my portable computer down now and concentrate on my driving.

Men who have a pierced ear are better prepared for marriage. They've experienced pain and bought jewelry.

EVERYTHING NEW IS
OLD AGAIN

Does anyone out there need a laser disc player? Make that three.

First eight-track tapes, then Betamax, and now this. When I switched my VHS collection to laser disc, no one had a clue that DVDs would soon take over the world. There was also no indication that VHS tapes would stick around and laser discs would become technological lepers. Now I'm frozen in electronic indecision. My husband has of course taken the leap and now is trying to convince me to repurchase all of our favorite movies in the DVD format, but I know in my heart that DVDs will not be around to see my daughter marry.

My distrust of buying anything electronic is now deeper than the frown line between my brows, and that, before Botox, was mighty deep. Do I really need a cell phone that takes pictures? I don't think so. I also don't need a camera that phones people up.

I don't need battery-powered sneakers, eyeglasses that get e-mail, or cars that can carry on a conversation. How can I persuade mankind to stop inventing needless gadgets that break down before they go out of style?

I have a friend who still owns a rotary phone. She keeps it in her closet so that no one who comes to visit her can see how old she really is, but she had the last laugh during the last New York blackout. When I called my friends to see if they were all right, she was the only one who answered.

"Not only am I fine," she said, "I'm the only person in New York who can dial out."

The other day, when my husband's electronic address book ran out of juice, he felt secure in knowing that all of his addresses were backed up in his computer.

"All I have to do is hot-sync it," he said. "No problem."

And it wouldn't have been, had he hot-synced the information from his computer into his electronic address book instead of the other way around.

"@%^$#*&, I can't believe it," he said. "I hot-synced the lack of information in my address book to my computer and it ate everything in the file."

"Ah," I said. I've learned that in situations like this, it is unwise to say more.

"Luckily, I've backed it up."

"Ah," I said again.

"@%^$#*&," he said again after extensive mouse clicking. "I've backed up everything in my computer except my address book. I didn't think I'd have to because I had it in two places."

"Ah," I repeated.

"I know," he stated confidently. "I have a program in my computer that can turn back time. I'll trick the computer into thinking it's yesterday."

"Ah."

"@%^$#*&, the last person who fixed the fan that cools my hard drive switched off that program. @%^$#*&," he added.

"Uh-huh," I uttered, feeling confident his recovery options were coming to an end.

"I'll call Brad. He'll know how to fix it."

Brad is a twenty-two-year-old who works in my theater. He knows everything about computers. If anyone could fix this problem, it was Brad.

"Have you looked in the recycle bin?" Brad asked. "Anything that's deleted should be in the recycle bin."

"Brad, you're a genius," my husband chortled even before he checked out Brad's theory.

"That @%^$#*& Brad knows nothing," my husband belched after checking the very empty recycle bin.

"Honey, I think you have to let it go," I volunteered. "We didn't like most of the people in your address book anyway."

"But it's everybody I've ever known in my life. They've disappeared into cyberspace and I'll never know how to get in touch with them again."

"You've got to take it easy. You don't need to contact your drama teacher from elementary school. You haven't talked to him for over thirty years. That part of your life is over. And besides, I have my address book right here, so we can always stay in touch with all of my friends."

"I liked it better when you just kept saying 'Ah,' " he snarled.

Giving up is not part of my husband's makeup.

"I've had another idea," he said later.

"Ah."

"Maybe I can turn the computer back to a month ago, which was before all this @%^$#*& happened. The computer will have to have a memory of the addresses then."

I held my breath while the search-and-recovery mission was implemented. I heard many noises emanate from my husband, and none of them could be interpreted as positive.

"I did it."

"What did you do?"

"I'm not sure. I think I annoyed my computer so badly it gave up. Look," he exclaimed, "the date on the computer is yesterday. I did it. I'm again able to contact hundreds of people I don't want to talk to."

"Congratulations, sweetheart. I knew you could do it."

"How about a victory celebration for your genius husband? Is there anything for lunch?"

I thought of the lasagna that had been in the refrigerator twenty-four hours ago.

"Is there any way you can trick the refrigerator into thinking it's yesterday?"

THINGS THAT AMAZE ME

1. How little meat is actually in a lamb chop.
2. How long half an hour can be when you're watching a bad television show.
3. How short half an hour can be when you're having a good time.
4. How many people still smoke.
5. How many thousands of people gather every New Year's Eve in Times Square in the freezing cold to watch a ball drop.

FISHY FRIENDS

Trying to make new friends after the age of forty is a little like eating my mother's cooking; it requires a lot of luck and a very strong stomach. Martin and I ventured out into new-friend-land a few times in our forties and came up with a combination of some very nice new people and some new adventures. My favorite adventure involved Mexico, fish tacos, and parrots.

We met Jack and Penny at a racecourse and had lunch with them a few times. Jack owned racehorses and Penny was a nurse. They invited us over to their house for dinner and we reciprocated.

"What a beautiful house," Peggy gushed.

"I love this furniture," Jack added. "You know, you can get a lot of this stuff much cheaper in Mexico."

I bridled somewhat, because we had recently spent a great deal of money on decorating and had never crossed the border.

Jack admired a very expensive bit of furniture we had purchased not long before. "That's a beautiful armoire. Penny, didn't we see something like that in Tijuana?"

"It's a hundred and ten inches tall and fifty inches wide. How would I get it back to Beverly Hills? On a team of donkeys?" I commented spikily.

"Believe me, they have really cheap delivery services down there," Jack assured me.

I could take it no more. I had to find out if we could have purchased all of our furniture for half the price in Mexico. We arranged our trip. I had a gig already booked in San Diego the following week, so we decided to meet Jack and Penny there. We would take Jack's car because he was familiar with the roads and spoke Spanish.

The trip did not begin well. We met Jack and Penny on a San Diego side street at 8:00 a.m.

"I apologize for the smell in the car," Jack explained. "My son and I went fishing yesterday and we brought home a bunch of salmon in the trunk. I've saved one for you."

Martin and I entered the fish car. Penny was already seated in the front.

"After a while you don't even notice it,"

she assured us.

We crossed over into Mexico and entered the furniture mecca that is Tijuana. Store after store offered nothing except wooden birds and papier-mâché fruit.

"I don't understand this," exclaimed a perplexed Jack. "Last time we were here we saw lots of stuff like yours. Isn't this something like your coffee table?"

"No, it's nothing like it," I replied happily.

"I heard you can buy some great cigars in Tijuana. Do you know anything about that, Jack?" Martin asked.

"Absolutely. You leave it to me. I speak Spanish. I'll bargain them down," Jack replied, evidently eager to save his Mexico reputation.

We located a small cigar store on the corner. Jack took charge.

"Señor. Cigaro. How mucho?"

So much for Jack's Spanish expertise. Jack purchased two cigars of questionable quality for about five dollars apiece after haggling in broken English for fifteen minutes.

"Anybody hungry? I know a great place to eat."

Jack led us to his favorite fish taco stand. Martin and I watched as he and Penny devoured the suspicious concoctions.

"I have a surprise for you. Tonight we're

going to stay overnight in our favorite hotel on the beach. My treat."

"W-well, thank you so much, but we have a room booked in San Diego for tonight," I stammered. Obviously it was a little too early for a playdate with this couple, let alone a sleepover.

"What's the number? I'll cancel it for you. I don't want you to miss out on an experience like this."

Jack drove deep into Mexico before I noticed that his gas gauge was nearing empty.

"Jack, you might want to fill up your tank. My treat," I offered.

"I've got plenty left," he replied confidently.

"There's a gas station right there," I pointed out. "Let's stop."

"I know a gas station that's much cheaper. Don't you worry."

Martin and I worried in the backseat as we witnessed the emergency you-better-fill-up-your-gas-tank light come on.

The car slowed as Jack looked around the shuttered gas station.

"It's been a while since I was here. I guess they closed this place down. Don't worry. I know another one not far down the road."

We sputtered to a gas station and filled up

the thirsty car. We drove another hour down the coast before pulling into the parking lot of an attractive hotel.

"This looks like a very nice place," I said with relief.

Jack was puzzled. "This parking lot is never full. I don't understand it."

"You made a reservation, didn't you, Jack?" Penny asked.

"You don't need a reservation at this place. They always have rooms."

Jack exited the car. He returned moments later. "Full tonight. They have lots of rooms tomorrow night."

Martin chimed in. "This has been quite an adventure, but it's getting dark and we're deep inside Mexico. Just for fun, let's not sleep in the car and get murdered tonight. Let's go home. We still have our hotel booked in San Diego."

"Oh, I canceled that," Jack said proudly.

"Don't worry," Martin whispered to me. "I had a feeling. I rebooked it."

We began our journey back to the border, but not before we got so lost we ended up in a small town that seemed to specialize in selling used parrots by the side of the road.

Penny the nurse gave me some career advice on the way back about what television shows I should appear on and why, which I always enjoy. When we arrived at the hotel in San Diego it was after 8:00 p.m. and Jack tried to book a room. Due to the ophthalmology convention, every hotel in town was full. Jack and Penny drove back to Glendale, and we returned to our room and celebrated the fact that we would never see Jack and Penny again.

Our friend foray in our forties had failed miserably, but I had proved to myself that I didn't overspend on our furniture. I did, however, have to throw away the outfit I wore on the trip. It always smelled of fish.

My husband came home with a staple gun the other day. He staple-gunned everything. There is nothing loose in our home anymore. There are a few major changes. For instance, now we have to bring the food to the cat.

GINBOREE

There are few things in life that I enjoyed more than taking my then-two-year-old daughter, Molly, to Gymboree. I was an only child and spent a lot of time talking to myself in a mirror. One of my earliest memories is arriving at kindergarten, looking around, and thinking, *Who are all these little people and why are they sharing toys?* So I felt the need to break the news to Molly early on in her life that there are other children in the world.

Once she could walk, I began taking Molly to organized activities, and she grew from a baby who was reluctant to participate into a gregarious toddler who would slide, stomp, and pop bubbles with the best of them. Everything was moving smoothly until a new parent moved into my Friday morning class.

The first indication that there was something amiss occurred while Sean, the father of Molly's friend Elise, and I attempted to help our daughters put together a Jimbo puzzle. This is trickier than it first appears. Jimbo wears many colors and not all of them live comfortably side by side. I was explaining the concept of finding all the straight pieces first and building a frame and Molly and Elise had begun handing me the straight bits when a small, round boy came and stomped on all we had accomplished.

I looked around to see if I could find someone who looked concerned enough to be his parent but could spot no one. The little boy then reached over and grabbed a piece of the puzzle out of Molly's hand. Molly, not having brothers or sisters to practice on, did not fight back. She just looked at me with sad blue eyes and said, "Mommy?" I looked around again but still could see no one responsible for the child. I took the piece of puzzle back from the little boy and gently said, "We're putting the puzzle together now, but in a minute you can rip it apart." Elise's father said nothing. In retrospect, I think he knew better.

It was then that *he* appeared from behind the green slide. His dark brown eyes matched his socks. It was a sartorial pity that his shorts and shirt didn't behave in the same way. He scooped up his little boy, shot me an eye bullet, and turned away.

"Do you know him?" I asked Sean.

"No, he's new in town, but I'm getting some strange vibes. He could be a psycho-dad."

"What's a psycho-dad?" I asked, putting Molly on the one slide she could manage by herself.

Before Sean could answer, Molly was met halfway down the slide by the same small, round boy climbing *up* the slide. They crashed into each other midway, which resulted in crying on both ends. Psycho-Dad again appeared, this time from behind the rainbow barrel, and scooped his child off the slide. Once more, he shot me a malevolent stare.

This time I just had to say something.

"I'm sure the child going down the slide should have the right-of-way, don't you think?"

"No," he said deliberately, and walked away.

Sean, who had witnessed the collision, chimed in, but only after the coast was clear.

"Don't get involved. Just stay out of that kid's way."

I took Sean's advice and continued on with the serious business of rolling hoops until it was parachute time. Then something happened that I just couldn't ignore.

There are roughly thirty balls in the class, all different sizes and colors. Molly's favorite color is yellow, which makes sense because Mommy's favorite color is pink (she's already trouble). Molly was sitting on my lap in the parachute circle and we were singing about the frog and the lily pad when the small, round child appeared again.

He proceeded to rip the yellow ball out of Molly's hands. I could stand it no more. I took the ball back and said, "There are lots of other balls. Please go get one of them." Tubby ripped the ball out of Molly's grasp again. I took it back again. Just then, Psycho-Dad appeared from behind the basketball hoop, grabbed his child, and snarled menacingly, "Don't you ever handle my son again."

"What?"

"You heard me. Don't you ever touch my son again."

"I didn't touch him. I just took the ball back. And by the way, where were you when all this was happening? Smoking behind the trampoline?"

"I was right here."

"Why didn't you do anything? Why didn't you tell your son not to grab things?"

"He's a baby. He grabs things. What's your problem?"

I looked over at Sean. He was shaking his head. I could see the conversation was going nowhere, so I joined into a chorus of "Itsy Bitsy Spider" and tried to be very adult about the whole thing.

After class, Molly and I were on our way out the door when I noticed the man waiting with his child outside. Was he waiting for me? I didn't know, but I decided to approach him first to try to smooth things over. Being a performer, I really hate when people don't like me.

"Look, this is silly," I began.

"You're aggressive," he interrupted. "You were aggressive with my child. Don't you ever go near him again . . . or else."

"OK, now you're threatening me. Now we have to go back into Gymboree and get counseling. Follow me."

We stomped back in, and I approached Philip, the Gymboree receptionist.

"Philip, I don't know what to do. I come to Gymboree, I wind up talking to O.J. He says I can't ever touch his child again 'or else.' "

"That's right," said Psycho-Dad menacingly.

"I didn't touch your child. I don't *want* to

touch your child," I told Psycho-Dad emphatically. "I want you to set boundaries for your child so I don't have to get involved."

Sean, bless him, then chimed in supportively.

"She's right. He doesn't set boundaries. He knocked Elise over on the stomping board today."

Another parent whom I didn't know also offered up a negative experience.

"I saw him throw a beanbag at another child. This guy just stood there and watched."

Three other Gymboree parents who had witnessed the puzzle and slide incidents sided with me.

Psycho-Dad had his own opinion.

"You're all crazy. I want my money back. I'm not bringing my son to a place where people manhandle him."

Philip gave him his money back and we never saw Psycho-Dad again.

I love being married. It's so great to find that one special person you want to annoy for the rest of your life.

FATHER DAYS

Being the only child of an aging parent comes with inevitable responsibility. I knew that one day my weekly phone call to Miami wouldn't be sufficient and I would be welcoming my colorful father back into my daily life. The move actually came at my suggestion. With my father's eyesight failing and his driver's license still valid, both my husband and I felt it was time to shift my elderly relative and his limited wardrobe to Las Vegas.

I anticipated an automatic no from my father followed by many hours of coaxing to facilitate this major life change. To my surprise, my dad jumped at the suggestion.

"I'll be there next week," he said enthusiastically.

"Well, first let's get all of our ducks in a row," I replied. "You have to sell your house and we have to rent you a place in Vegas."

He saw the sense in this. "OK, I'll be there

in two weeks."

The real estate market was in a good mood and the old house that I grew up in sold within a month. I had been six years old when we first moved into the brand-new house, and now, forty years later, it was time for the Rudner clan to officially leave the building. Our house had gone from being the best house in a bad neighborhood to the worst one in a good neighborhood. At this point my father's castle wasn't as much a tear-down as it was a blow-down. I don't know who bought his house, but unless it was a family of termites, I apologize.

My father had never married again after the death of my stepmother and had lived alone for the last twenty-five years. Even the sanest person allowed to live alone for a quarter of a century will develop a few idiosyncrasies, and my dad was never one to be called sane.

The first clue as to how strange he had become were the boxes that arrived for us to unpack a few weeks before his arrival.

"Martin," I inquired of my husband as I scrutinized the contents of the package, "why is my father mailing cans of pineapple juice?"

"I don't know," Martin replied, staring into his opened box. "I've got baked beans in here."

Box after box was stuffed with canned juices and beans. Dirty shirts and socks were intermittently wedged between them to keep them secure.

"Look at the date on this V-8 juice," I exclaimed. "January sixth, 1992. He's drinking ten-year-old tomato juice."

My husband looked at the date on the can he was holding. "That goes nicely with a twelve-year-old can of baked beans."

Not every box was filled with canned goods. One package contained rusty tools and ten boxes of freezer wrap. Another contained thirty tubes of toothpaste intermingled with forty tubes of antifungal cream. My dad was a hoardaholic.

My father loved the apartment we had rented for him. It was a perfect situation. We lived in the building next door, so we could be there if he needed us, and we could also pretend we were away.

I became his professional grocery shopper, which was how I discovered how much he was drinking. His first shopping list included four gallons of Zinfandel, three bottles of scotch, ten boxes of Kleenex, a dozen bottles of rubbing alcohol, and a request for more antifungal cream.

"What about food?" I asked.

"I packed that in the boxes."

I broke the news to him that although I had been tempted to sell his canned goods on eBay under the heading "antique food," his carefully packed groceries were now living happily with their friends in the garbage dump.

Attempting to change a diet that obviously had consisted of rusty juices and rotten beans for at least a decade was quite a challenge. I included TV dinners, fruits, and vegetables in his first grocery delivery and introduced him to the microwave.

The first time he attempted to use the microwave, instead of entering nine minutes he mistakenly entered ninety. The explosion broke the seal of the microwave and a brown gooey mixture ran down the front of the cabinetry. That Salisbury steak TV dinner left a stain that will still be there long after all of us are gone.

His drinking represented another issue. His reasoning made sense. He was eighty-two. He didn't drive, he didn't work, he didn't have to be anywhere at any given time, and he liked to sleep. What was wrong with drinking scotch in the morning? It was positively healthy! He used it to down his vitamin pills. A glass of wine with his lunch didn't sound all that unreasonable until you factored in that lunch occurred at ten o'clock and the wineglass was a ten-ounce tumbler.

Still, the relocation had been a success. Dad took daily walks during the couple of hours in the afternoon when he was sober, and our then-one-and-a-half-year-old daughter loved to visit him in the next building. She even got him to play a game she invented, called Hats. She noticed some baseball caps on his coffee table and with baby sign language demanded we put them on our heads and rotate them when she yelled "hat."

I noticed my father limping slightly on one of his walks, and when I asked him about it he complained that something was "sticking in his foot." Back up at his apartment I found myself in shock when I saw what was going on at the base of his body. This man who carefully applied antifungal cream to his toes every single day had not cut his toenails in years. My father had Howard Hughes's feet.

"What's going on? Why don't you cut your toenails?" I asked.

"Can't see down there."

"How are you applying the antifungal cream?"

"Badly, but I have to do it. You get athlete's

foot, it's with you for life."

"You've lived alone for almost thirty years. Who are you going to get athlete's foot from? Mice?"

"You never know. Some of these germs are airborne."

I decided not to argue with a man who even in his youth had made very little sense. Not only was I his personal grocery shopper, but now I was also his pedicurist.

All was going relatively smoothly until my father's diet caught up with him. One morning during our daily phone call I asked him, "How're you doing?" and he replied that his stomach wasn't "so hot."

I rushed over to find him leaning back on the couch, his face a shade of statue gray.

"Just wait a couple hours. I'll be OK," he mumbled.

I hadn't listened to him when I was a teenager and I didn't listen to him then. I called an ambulance.

Acute diverticulitis was the least of his problems. Once his condition was stabilized, an X-ray revealed an aneurysm in his aorta that was poised to burst. The doctors recommended an operation that, although it would be difficult to recover from, had a very high success rate. It was up to my father whether or not he wanted to go through the invasive procedure and the rigorous physical therapy that would be required post-op.

He chose the operation. It was as they had promised: successful and debilitating. My father was never one to exert himself, and the rehabilitation therapist had quite a time convincing him that getting out of bed tomorrow was not optional.

When he was discharged I was told what foods should be given to him and that his drinking had to stop. He was given a strict exercise regime that he immediately ignored. Without the foods he liked or the drink he craved, and unable to motivate himself even to get out of his pajamas, he sank speedily into a deep depression that ultimately won.

My father's life-threatening aneurysm was gone, but he was never happy again. I tried everything. Even my daughter could no longer bring a smile to his face. He died one night in his sleep and no one could figure out why. He'd been to the doctor and been checked out a few days before, and had been prescribed an increased dose of antidepressants. The doctor wrote "heart attack" on his death certificate because he didn't know what else to write. I think my father died because he wanted to. Ironic, when you consider the pain and expense he suffered when he was informed he possessed a life-threatening condition.

It had been my father's decision to undergo the operation. I didn't try to sway him one way or the other. I didn't want the guilt fairy visiting me for the rest of my life and scolding me for persuading him to make the wrong decision.

I do know the right decision had been for me to move him to Las Vegas in his old age and look after him the best I could. I knew every inch of my father by the time he died: the good, the bad, and the toenails.

It did leave me thinking about the way I'll handle my old age. If there's a choice of having a few weeks of fun rather than six months of hell, I'll be having the martini.

'TWAS THE NIGHT
AFTER CHRISTMAS

'Twas the night after Christmas and back
   in the kitchen
The family was sittin' and drinkin' and
   bitchin'.
My husband in his robe and me in my shift
Discuss and debate whom and what to
   regift.
Old Aunt Sophie gave me money; is she
   lazy or wary?
Why did Grandma give me shoes that
   would fit a canary?
It's not only them. I am also pathetic:
I gave Grandpa chocolate and he's
   diabetic.
My daughter still asks why she can't ride
   her bike
(It came unassembled, so she may have to
   hike).
With instructions in Japanese, Spanish, and
   Mayan,

It might never work, but we won't stop
  tryin'.
Martin hates his new jacket and he wants
  to burn it.
I soon calm him down and agree to return
  it.
But I've cleared up the box in my quest to
  be neat
And it seems accidentally I've tossed the
  receipt.
My overcooked turkey's caused us all
  indigestion.
We retire to bed with our sanity in
  question.
One thing we agree on before we all say
  good night:
We're glad Christmas is over as we turn off
  the light.

If Not Now, When?

You know you're getting old when you begin looking for places to live when you retire. Martin and I began looking for places to retire when we were on our honeymoon. Although we were only in our thirties, it seemed like a good idea to plan for the future. We had our post-wedding vacation at the Ritz-Carlton Hotel in Dana Point, California. We were so low on funds we had booked a room overlooking the pool rather than the ocean, but upon hearing that it was our honeymoon, the management took pity on us and upgraded our room to a suite on the ocean.

Martin and I enjoyed just-married morning coffee on our beachfront balcony and luxuriated in the ocean breeze. We watched the dolphins playing in the waves and the boats sailing by on the horizon.

"This is where I want to retire," Martin said.

"Me too," I replied. "Let's save our money and try to buy this balcony."

As luck would have it, a community was being developed directly next door to the hotel. The lots had been outlined with little yellow flags and the development's representative was happy to show us the different options that were available. He also shared with us the prices of each oblong of dirt. Martin and I tried not to laugh as he explained the fantastic value that was to be had for merely hundreds of thousands of dollars.

For now the dolphins could afford to live in Dana Point, but we would have to wait. We put our retirement fantasy on hold and set out to earn some money.

Five years later, we returned to the Ritz-Carlton for a weekend and tried again. This time we sauntered down the road and located an unsuspecting real estate agent named Beverly whom we would subsequently drive crazy over the next twelve years.

"You don't want to see the properties next to the Ritz-Carlton," Beverly informed us. "They've tripled in value in the past five years."

Martin and I remained silent and nauseated. Beverly showed us a few properties that we could almost afford. They were pleasant and a stone's throw away from the beach if you could throw a stone ten miles. It just didn't make sense to us to buy a beach house that was so far away from the beach. We thanked Beverly and assured her that we wouldn't be bothering her again.

A few years later, Martin and I bought a vacation house in Palm Desert on a golf course. People don't go into retirement and then decide to play golf; golf takes so long to play you have to go into retirement to play it. We went into semi-retirement in our forties and only played nine holes. It was a modest yet idyllic house. It looked out on a lake and a mountain that were so perfect it was as if someone came out each day and polished them. It was lovely, but we still harbored a secret desire to have a house on the ocean. And Beverly, bless her masochistic heart, was still sending us brochures for beach-frontish property.

When Martin and I moved to Las Vegas, the house in Palm Desert stopped making sense. In the summer when it was 110 degrees in Vegas, it was 120 degrees in Palm Desert.

"Rita," Martin said one day, "it occurs to me that we have two houses in places that are hotter than the sun."

We had officially come out of semi-retirement anyway, and with a steady job in Las Vegas and a baby on the way, smacking a tiny white ball into a hole for five hours at a time was no longer a priority.

Beverly had some new properties to show us. The first was the inside-out house. The bedroom was on the first floor and the living room was upstairs. It had a beautiful view from the living room and the bedroom looked at a wall.

The second house was so far up a mountain I thought we might be eaten by bears. The third was perfect. Recently renovated and Tuscan in feel, it overlooked the ocean and boasted a backyard with a fire pit and barbecue.

Dan, the real estate agent representing the seller of the house that Beverly had found for us, was adamant that Martin and I should buy it.

"If not now, when?" he said.

"Maybe when we can afford it," I replied.

"When you can afford it, it will be out of your price range," he stated wisely.

We had learned from our first mistake when we didn't buy the land next to the Ritz-Carlton. Oceanfront property tends to go up in value. We agreed to meet Dan later with an offer. Over drinks at a swanky hotel,

Dan began going over some minor details associated with the property.

"The thing about this house that I really like," he said, smiling, "is that in 2020, you'll be able to buy the land at only sixty percent of its value."

"Could you please repeat that?" asked Martin.

"The land is owned by a trust and comes up for sale in 2020," Dan repeated.

"So this property is already out of our price range, and if we buy it, we don't own the land," Martin stated.

"Exactly!"

"So, where don't I sign?" I said, handing the paperwork back to Dan.

We returned to Las Vegas, resolving never to try to buy property in Dana Point again.

Beverly waited a few years until we calmed down and then gave us a call.

"I think I've found something for you. It's not on the market yet. It's a renovation and you could get it before they decide on materials. You could get it exactly the way you want."

We couldn't resist. We met Beverly at her office and reminisced about all that had occurred since we first entered her life. I had become a mother, she had become a grandmother. She had remarried, and Martin and

I were now celebrating our fourteenth anniversary. We followed her to the house where we could help choose the materials.

The house required a complete renovation. It would take years for the planning permission and requisite architectural approval, and my gray hair was already becoming dye-resistant. The beach was within walking distance and an easy journey if you were a mountain goat. We felt bad for Beverly, but it was a no.

Beverly had another house up her sleeve. It was in the area we'd first seen sixteen years before. It was within walking distance of a beach and it was something we could afford. It was a starter house with an ocean peek.

"See the ocean through that vacant lot? There is very little chance anyone would ever build on that lot and block your view," Beverly promised.

Martin and I shook our heads.

"I've got one more," she said.

"Beverly, you have to stop now. I can't torture you any longer."

"Rita, at this point it's not even a job anymore. I'm on a mission. I will not rest until I find you and Martin a house."

We followed Beverly into a beautiful neighborhood and pulled up in front of an understated contemporary house that was exactly what Martin and I were looking for.

"This house fell out of escrow yesterday," Beverly explained. "I think it's meant to be."

Martin and I wandered into the living room. The sliding glass doors opened up into the walls and the breeze wafted through the living room. It had everything we were looking for. It was big enough but not too big, and easy walking distance to the beach.

Martin and I looked at each other and said, "If not now, when?"

We made an offer on the house that afternoon, and it was accepted. We went out with Beverly and bought her a well-deserved drink.

It had taken seventeen years, but Martin and I had finally bought our dream house. It's the house we always wanted and never thought we could find. There is only one problem . . . we don't own the land.

I really wanted a child. I didn't want to be old and sick and not have someone to drain financially.

It's My Daughter's Party and I'll Cry if I Want To

Typical Vegas parties usually feature names like Paris Hilton and Lindsay Lohan and always occur at the hippest hangouts in town. Don't think Martin and I haven't checked out these nightclubs, because we have . . . but only during the day. Being the proud parents of a toddler and a dog on diuretics leaves us roughly six hours of interrupted sleep a night, so clubbing with the beautiful people is quite simply a non-starter. That's not to say we're not party people. We are.

When Martin and I adopted our baby girl everybody warned me about no sleep, tantrums, and potty training; nobody warned me about birthday parties. It seems that each child my daughter knows has at least three birthday parties a year. We have been to bouncing parties, ice-skating parties, Build-a-Bear parties, dress-up parties, cookie-making parties, and horseback-riding parties, and that was just last week. This is the story of my daughter's party and why after it was over I needed a drink.

Celebrating birthdays one through three had been a breeze. At these ages children's frames of reference are rather narrow; they don't have many friends and haven't really experienced a full-blown celebration. We got off easily. We bought a cake and hats and invited some strangers, and Molly was totally satisfied. At four everything changes.

"Mommy, Krystal had pony rides at her birthday party. What am I going to have?"

"Well, honey, we have a dog on diuretics. I'm pretty sure he's available," I replied.

That answer didn't fly. Four was going to be a very different experience compared to one, two, and three.

The planning of a child's birthday party becomes significantly more difficult when you live in an apartment. Ponies are out of the question, as are pigs, donkeys, and any other animal that has a relationship with hay. While our child's bedroom is fair game for stickers, Play-Doh, and grape juice, our mohair living room sofa is not up to having a gaggle of four-year-olds partying on its pampered cushions.

Outside was calling and we were answering the phone. We would organize the party around the apartment complex's pool. The catering department was happy to oblige and overcharge us. We had the hamburgers and hot dogs planned along with iced tea and lemonade, but what were the little darlings going to do all afternoon? Half of them didn't know how to swim yet, so pushing them into the pool wasn't really an option. Children seem to like to jump, so we rented a bouncy castle to tire them out. We hired a Cinderella look-alike to paint the children's faces and twist balloons into unnatural positions.

Invitations were issued and I waited patiently by the phone for the RSVPs to fly in.

One day, two days, three days passed and no one bothered to respond. I could wait no longer. I tackled some of my daughter's friends' mothers in the playground. There was a slight problem in that I didn't know any of their names.

"Excuse me, Krystal's mother," I said. "Is Krystal going to be able to come to Molly's birthday party?"

"Sure, Molly's mother," she said. "Krystal is going to come with Dixie. We're looking forward to it."

I did the same with Tess's mother and Bella's mother. They were all coming; they just hadn't responded yet. Maybe I shouldn't have sent out the invitations a month in advance. I just wanted the first birthday party that my daughter would remember to be special, and special it was.

I don't know whether it was something she ate or a bug she picked up at school, but the morning of the party began with my daughter vomiting copiously all over the house (don't worry, the mohair sofa was not hit). The every-ten-minutes vomiting was not our only problem. The hottest day of the year was forecast, and for once the forecast was correct. At noon, we took our ailing daughter downstairs to greet seven friends and 110 degrees.

I have never been prouder of Molly. Pausing only to throw up in the lobby downstairs, she got through the entire party like a trouper. I hesitate to say this in Las Vegas, but Cinderella's balloons were magnificent. The bouncy house was a triumph, even though my daughter only ventured inside for the benefit of a single photo op. The food was great, although perhaps we didn't need the barbecue — we could have let the meat cook in the sun. The piñata ended the party with a flourish and everyone went home happy and on a sugar high.

My husband and I woke up the next

morning as though we had both been beaten with sticks. Our daughter bounced into our room, completely recovered.

"Are we having another party today?" she asked brightly.

"Not today, but soon."

"How soon?"

"As soon as you're eighteen."

I was a very introverted child. I only had two friends. And they were imaginary. And they would only play with each other.

THE KNEE-JERK NO

When I was first studying comedy, one of the most important things I learned was in an improv class. Ironically, it helped me even more in my life than in my act. The thing that I learned was simple and obvious, but I'm going to tell it to you anyway because I see so many people not doing it.

Here it is . . . drumroll, please . . . Saying yes gets you further than saying no.

Sure, saying yes can get you into trouble. I'm not advocating saying yes to drugs, to promiscuous sex, or to infomercials. I'm advocating saying yes to change and possibilities.

The knee-jerk no is definitely something to avoid. Whenever I'm inclined to say no, I ask myself, "Do I have a reason that I'm saying no to this or is it just out of habit?"

I have a very good friend whose life has not progressed in the way she would have liked. Whenever I've tried to help her redirect her life toward a different path, she says no and continues along the same well-beaten route. I have heard *insanity* defined as "repeating the same behavior and expecting a different result." I know that having the courage to change something is more productive than staying the course. I firmly believe that if you want your situation to change, you have to change your situation. When I review my life thus far, I can see that's one of the things I did right. Changing careers, houses, cities — all of these have gotten me to a place that I love but which I know will eventually change once again.

Switching from dancing to comedy was a rational decision. I noticed that George Burns was still working, while Gene Kelly hadn't had a gig in quite some time. As a dancer, you have a few choices you can make as you age. You can go back to school, you can teach dancing, you can marry someone who has a job where they don't have to jump around, or you can insist on loitering in a profession that is meant for young people, make no money, and eat cat food.

I was a confirmed New Yorker. I never thought I would leave. When I got a call from a comedy producer to play the Edinburgh Festival in Scotland, I was very tempted to say no. I was steeped in a routine that could not be altered. How could I possibly not swim a hundred laps four mornings a week and not attend ballet class every morning at 10:00 a.m.? How would I survive?

Luckily, two of my comedy friends were also asked to be in the show, and they talked me into it. I reasoned it would only be for three weeks, we would have fun, and I wouldn't turn to complete flab in twenty-one days. Just in case, I had the producer of the show (who later became my husband) scout out an Olympic-sized pool and a local ballet class before I would give them a definite yes.

Edinburgh is one of the most beautiful cities on earth, part medieval and part Georgian, with a castle perched above the town and flower boxes seemingly decorating every window. I swam twice and took a few ballet classes before I abandoned rigid discipline and opted for sightseeing and socializing. After the three weeks were up, I returned to New York culturally richer and none the flabbier.

Most important, I met the man who would later become my husband. For all you women out there who are looking for someone to share your life with, the first thing I would suggest is to throw away the list of things you require from a potential mate. I once dated a man who was walking perfection. He had everything on the list — he was handsome, smart, athletic, personable, heterosexual, and single. One problem: he was the most selfish individual I've ever known. If he wanted to do something, he would do it. If he wanted to go somewhere, he was gone. Most of all, if he wanted to sleep with another woman, you would just have to deal with it. I don't know if he ever married, but I always said, "He is going to make some lucky girl very unhappy."

When the producer of the Edinburgh show called and asked me to perform in Australia, I said yes. Australia was a bit scarier; it was so far away I had to buy an extension for my map. However, I'd had such a good time in Scotland, I figured what was the worst that could happen? Even if the show bombed, I'd still accrue a huge amount of frequent-flyer miles. The show did in fact bomb, but I didn't care. I got engaged and stayed in Australia a month longer than I originally planned. I'd never thought I would marry someone who lived on another continent, who was in show business, and who was younger than I was. But we're celebrating our nineteenth anniversary all because I said yes instead of the dreaded knee-jerk no.

Beware — the knee-jerk no sometimes reappears after you say yes. I have another friend who hated her hair. She said it was too dark and too thin, and she hated the style. I had a hairdresser whom I loved in L.A. I took my friend in and said, "Work your magic." My friend emerged from her hair therapy a new woman. The stylist had lightened her hair to lesson the hair/scalp contrast, layered it to make it softer, and blown it dry so my friend wouldn't have to set it in huge rollers and be mistaken for an alien. My friend loved it. A couple of months later my friend sent me a picture of herself at her birthday party and I saw that her hair was back exactly the way it had been when she hated it. I asked her why, and she told me she felt the other hairdo was good for a change, but her original style covered the wrinkles in her forehead and made her look younger. As in the aftermath of rehab, the potential to go back to behavior that is comfortable is always looming.

The biggest change that my husband and I made was moving out of Los Angeles and adopting a baby. When we first arrived in Los Angeles everything was new and possible, and we had lots of fun doing things we'd never believed we would ever do. Writing movies, performing on television shows, and attending those award ceremonies that you see on television and think look glamorous were all exciting and excruciating.

I know this isn't going to shock you, but Los Angeles is not a place for entertainers to age. One day my husband and I looked at the new fall television lineup and noticed that Christina Applegate was appearing in a sitcom playing a divorced mother of two. At that point she was still safely in her twenties. If I stayed in Hollywood for a few more years, there was a shot that while still in my forties, I could play a great-grandmother. It was time to move.

We looked around at the possibilities. Las Vegas had always been a staple of my career. I had been headlining casinos there for the past decade and we always looked forward to our trips. It was then that my producer husband came up with the idea of a permanent show on the Strip instead of just headlining for a few weeks a year. That was a move that was as dramatic as it was terrifying. We'd also been talking about adopting a baby. We said yes to both and changed our lives for the better in more ways than you can cook chicken.

I have to admit saying yes has also caused

me to invest money with a person who had a fictional business, try foods that have made me sick, and date someone who was eventually shot by the police, but the ways it has improved my life are too numerous to mention.

Now, again, my point is not to say yes to everything. My point is to examine why you're saying no, and if you're saying no automatically because that's what you're used to saying, rethink it. You might find yourself in a better situation.

More things can come through an open window than through a closed door. There, I'm officially out of aphorisms. I'm going to stop now. I'm sounding like a Japanese psychiatrist.

Before I met my husband, I'd never fallen in love. I'd stepped in it a few times.

Overpaying Your Dues

"Welcome to the neighborhood," the casually dressed man slurred, holding up a glass of white wine. It was our first day in our new house and Martin and I were bleary-eyed from unpacking mislabeled boxes.

"I'm Mitch Kemp," the man continued. "I'm the president of Sycamore Road. Just wanted to introduce myself . . . I take care of everything that you need. I've lived on Sycamore for twenty-five years. If you have any questions about how this street works, you just ask me."

"I have a question," I asked. "How do we get clickers to raise and lower the gates?"

"I'll take care of that," Mitch replied confidently. "In the meantime, here is the code — just punch it in. The code is changed every three months for security reasons."

"What a nice man," I said as he walked away.

"He wants money," my husband muttered under his breath.

I have to explain that Sycamore Road is a private street. To stop hurried drivers from using it as a shortcut, it was gated at both ends, and as a result it's now no longer the city's responsibility.

My suspicious husband turned out to be right. A few days later a bill arrived in our mailbox. It wasn't for a lot of money: $125 every three months. With it, we received a list of all the people on Sycamore Road and their phone numbers. Stars were next to the names of residents who had paid the fee. There was an X next to the names of those who were delinquent.

"What does he do for these dues?" my husband complained, mentally adding up how much money this came to each year.

"He takes care of the road," I explained.

"What does he take care of?"

"He makes sure it's OK."

"Does he feed it? Does he take it to the movies? It's a road. What does he do that requires forty thousand dollars a year?"

"Let's just pay him. We don't want an X next to our names; we want a star."

The next day the clickers that controlled the movement of the street gates appeared in our mailbox.

"See, he gave us clickers," I said excitedly, happy to have evidence that we were getting something for our dues.

"Wait a second, what's this?" my husband questioned, pulling out a sheet of paper from the envelope. "Fifty dollars? Fifty dollars for clickers? Where is the bill that shows us how much he paid for them?" he whined.

"He went and got the clickers. He has to be compensated for his time."

"I bet he's got a stack of them in his garage. He just wanted to make sure we paid our dues before he gave us the clickers. I'm not paying him for the clickers."

"We have to. We'll get an X."

Sycamore Road was a quaint little street. People jogged, dogs walked, deer even occasionally meandered through our backyard. One day I spotted Mitch stooping down and inspecting a crack in the pavement. I ran back home.

"I saw Mitch do something! He was inspecting a crack in the blacktop."

"That's going to cost more money," my husband insisted.

"No. That's what the dues are for. I promise. He takes care of the road."

In the following days, yellow Xs began to appear on all the cracks on the road.

"I guess the cracks didn't pay their dues," my husband quipped.

A note appeared in our mailbox: *The upper portion of the road will be repaved on the twenty-second of April and the lower portion on the twenty-fifth. Please use the opposite entrances.*

I was vindicated. There it was — proof that our money was being used for something tangible. What the note didn't mention was that the road was not the only thing being resurfaced; Mitch had also included his extensive driveway. This turned out to be something that a poker player would refer to as a "tell."

I was too timid to tackle him about it, and ultimately so was my husband. We just kept paying our dues and feeling slightly aggrieved.

Mitch Kemp died a few years later. He was the victim of a sudden heart attack. His wife was the one who was the most shocked. Mitch had not only kept all of the road money in a secret bank account, but he was using it to pay for his mistress in France. Unable to face the people on Sycamore Road, Mitch's wife put the house up for sale and moved away.

Turns out the people with Xs by their names had been right. If only I hadn't

wanted a star.
I blame my kindergarten teacher.

I never fully understand what goes on in dry cleaning. I know they add a safety pin.

THE SECOND ACT

My first writing partner was a woman named Marjorie Gross. In the early eighties, we were both just beginning to practice stand-up comedy. We were getting onstage very late at night or, in a positive light, very early in the morning, so we had lots of time to hang out and talk in the bar. I began watching Marjorie's stage set and she began watching mine.

Writing jokes isn't easy for anyone, so Marjorie and I decided to meet a few times a week and try to do it together.

The thing that's unusual about this is that Marjorie and I were about as different as left and right. We had no business writing together and it made even less sense that we were good friends. I was at that point in my life very structured and somewhat rigid; she was a total free spirit whose life swayed wildly depending on her mood. I was neat, she was sloppy; I was always on time, she was always late. We were Felix and Oscar, only we were both women. One of her favorite pastimes was tossing wet tea bags across the room to see if she could hit the garbage can. I think she missed on purpose. She liked the sound of the splat.

We had one thing in common: both of our mothers had died when we were in our early teens, mine from breast cancer and Marjorie's from ovarian. We vowed to be extra diligent to ensure that didn't happen to us.

There was no one funnier than Marjorie Gross. I would study the structure of writing jokes by listening to comedy albums, and she would just come out with thoughts that were totally unique. A typical joke-writing session would produce the following.

Rita: Doctors can tell a lot about a baby while it's still inside the womb these days. My friend is pregnant and it seems the baby is normal, and it's a boy, and it's a lawyer.

Marjorie: How do Chinese parents know when their babies are starting to talk?

Marjorie refused to do anything the way it should be done. Her apartment had been broken into repeatedly. Marjorie would call her answering machine once an hour not to check her messages but to make sure it was still there. Eventually she decided to take the law into her own hands. Instead of locking the window and having bars placed on the outside the way New Yorkers do, creating a kind of well-decorated prison, Marge bought a can of axle grease and smeared it over the window ledge. The burglar would simply repeatedly slip and fall when he tried to enter her third-floor premises.

I saw half of many Broadway shows with my friend Marjorie. It was she who taught me the art of second-acting.

"It's easy," she explained. "You just stand outside the theater at intermission and mingle with the audience, and when they let everyone back in for the second act you walk in with the real people."

"How do you know which seats are empty?" I asked stupidly.

"Rita, think. You go to the bathroom and wait till everyone is seated and then you find the empty chairs. Nobody cares. It's not like we're taking seats from other people. We're not even seeing the whole play. If we really like the second act, we can buy tickets and see the first. This will actually increase their business."

Our scam worked well until Marge got a

little cocky. We were second-acting *American Buffalo* when Marge decided to put her feet up on the chair in front of her and kicked a lady in the head. We were asked by an usher to show our tickets and were summarily shown the exit. That is the closest I've ever come to breaking the law.

Marge and I began writing sketches together. After we actually sold a few to a television show in Canada, we decided to audition to write for *Saturday Night Live*. Marjorie was very concerned that my clothing would not be hip enough and came to my house before our meeting to see if she could help me put together a few things that didn't match.

Our favorite audition sketch we'd written for *SNL* featured Snow White, Cinderella, and Sleeping Beauty, all divorced and all complaining about their princes. We didn't get the job, but Marjorie soon was hired to write on a television show in Los Angeles, and I began performing on the David Letterman show and *HBO*.

I received a call from Marjorie a few weeks after she moved to L.A. She had pitched our divorced princesses idea to a major studio and they wanted to commission her to write it . . . with somebody else. Of course I wanted to write it with her, but I had no credits and the woman she was working with had written movies. Looking back, I had a point and so did she. The conversation did not go well and we lost contact.

When I moved to L.A. a few years later, I ran into Marjorie at a comedy club and we immediately began laughing about the whole thing. She had written the movie, it had gotten stalled in development the way 99 percent of projects do, and she had always regretted our argument, as did I.

Our careers blossomed in different directions, hers as a writer and mine as a comedian. We remained good friends for years. One day I received a call from Marge. She was in New York writing on a new television show.

"Reetee," she said, "this television show I'm working on is so bad, I think it's given me cancer."

"What are you talking about?"

"I had this terrible pain in my stomach and I went to the gyno. She said it's not good."

The ovarian cancer that had invaded Marjorie's mother had shown up in Marge. She went back to Canada to have the operation. My heart sank when I talked to her dad on the phone and he told me, "They did their best, but they couldn't get all of it."

Marjorie came to stay with us while going through her first round of chemotherapy. It was challenging, but strangely always funny.

I'd be on my way out to the grocery store and would ask, "What can I get for you? Anything special?"

"Nah."

I'd return home with a full complement of food for the week, and Marge would wander into the kitchen. "Did you get any matzo?"

"No."

"I'm really in the mood for matzo. I'll call one of my friends. They'll bring it over."

We had a constant stream of people we didn't know wandering in and out of our house as well as the scent of marijuana regularly wafting up the stairs. I have never had anything to do with drugs, but to me, legalizing marijuana for people who are going through the agony of chemo is as easy a decision as letting nearsighted people wear glasses.

Marjorie was not happy with our collection of movies and demanded we obtain Oscar review copies from some of our friends who were members of the Academy. Once I heard strange noises coming from her bedroom. I peeked inside and Marjorie was listening to strangers' cell phone calls on a police radio.

"You've gotta hear this agent negotiating this contract. He is such a pig!"

"Marjorie, is this right? Listening to people's private calls?"

"Rita, I have cancer. What are they going to do to me that's worse than this?" she replied.

It was comforting knowing that Marjorie was just downstairs and we could be there in seconds if she really needed us. I loved sitting on the side of her bed as we ranted about the injustices of show business and commented on the current state of various celebrities' love lives.

After going into remission, Marge started working on *Seinfeld* and wrote a memorably funny episode starring Bette Midler. Always full of surprises, she called me one day from Donatella Versace's villa in Italy, where she had just been flown on Madonna's private jet.

"I'm here at the pool overlooking the manicured gardens. Madonna and Donatella thought it would be good for me to have a little vacation," she explained.

The cancer returned a few more times before taking her life. To her credit — or perhaps detriment — Marjorie never accepted the fact that she was going to die. The day before she passed away, she begged her doctor for one more round of chemo and was on the phone with her agent arguing about the finer points of her next year's contract with *Seinfeld.*

I often think of her and want to tell her everything that's been going on. I want to tell her that Martin and I adopted a baby girl and that two of her best friends have written a hit musical on Broadway. Most of all, I want to tell her that Howie Mandel is bald.

I know we all bitch about getting older and the state the world is in, but just to be able to wake up every day and live our second act is a privilege that we should never take for granted.

How come when you mix flour and water you get glue? And then you add eggs and sugar and you get cake. Where does the glue go?

On Your Mark, Get Set, Sit Down

As people age, it becomes more difficult for them to leave the house. My mother-in-law holds the current world record for getting ready. Many men read newspapers or watch television while their wives are primping and changing handbags; my father-in-law has time to solve crimes. In the four hours it takes his wife to make herself presentable to strangers, he can detect which neighbors are depositing their garbage in his can and which dog is relieving itself on his lawn. If you add up all of the time in their fifty-two years of marriage he has spent waiting for my mother-in-law to get ready, it comes to approximately 18,980 hours. I remind my husband of this whenever he complains that I'm taking too long to leave the house.

In my defense, I am not what you'd call an organized person. I don't write people down in alphabetical order in my address book. I write them down in the order in which I met them. It takes me a little longer to find their phone numbers, but it's more satisfying when I do because it requires skill.

Being a woman is difficult. It takes time, effort, and creativity. It's like being a female impersonator every single day. Men don't understand what takes so much time, and I feel it is my duty to the female sex to at least attempt to inform them of what is involved in our preparations on a daily basis.

Let us begin with makeup. We cleanse, we tone, we moisturize; we apply concealer, sunscreen, foundation, shading, and powder. Then we're ready to begin.

An eye-makeup primer is applied to the eye, either with a finger or a brush. Over that, a lighter color is applied on the inner eyelid and above the brow. At this point we may find stray eyebrow hairs that offend us and we may elect to pluck them. If this is the case, the above steps might have to be repeated. A deeper color is applied to the eyebrow crease using a tapered brush that might have to be cleaned and dried if we've chosen to apply a different color than the day before. This is followed by eyeliner that must be smudged for a natural effect, an eyelash-curling session, and mascara. If we sneeze before any of the above products are dry, we're looking at a restart.

Blush is applied sparingly to each cheek, beginning approximately one inch from the nose and stroked upward. It is then blended so the woman is not mistaken for a clown. The lips are lined in a color that will blend with our chosen lipstick. Thank heaven lining the mouth in a darker shade is a thing of the past. Not only was it symmetrically challenging, to me it made a woman's mouth look like a crime scene. We fill in our lips with a tiny brush so as to not overstep our lip boundaries, and then we are ready to tackle our hair.

Depending on the type of hair a woman has, the time of this part of the operation can vary greatly. A curly-haired woman attempting to masquerade as a straight-haired woman can take over an hour to achieve the follicle lie she is attempting to tell. In a humid climate, this effort will last for only a few minutes. However, the woman will never stop blow-drying and accept the hair for what it is. I know. I am this woman.

After hair, it's time to make the clothing decision. First, we have to evaluate if it is a fat or thin day. We then select accordingly. Our opening move is to stare blankly into a closet stuffed fuller than a clown car and lament that we have nothing to wear. If we zoom in on a dress, the next step will be over quickly. Should we be putting together an outfit, add on twenty minutes. We're going to try a few different jackets with our skirt or pants. If it is winter, tack on an additional forty minutes. We have to locate coats, scarves, and gloves.

The first pair of stockings we shimmy into will have a hole in them, and if we're not wearing slacks that day, they will have to be put back into the drawer and a new pair chosen.

Once we are dressed, an appropriate pair of shoes is selected depending on how much we intend to walk that day and whether or not we are going to lunch with someone we want to impress.

Jewelry takes a good chunk of time because the clasps are nearly impossible to fasten. Superman with his X-ray vision would need a magnifying glass to unite the two ends of my favorite necklace in less than ten minutes.

I've saved the handbag for last. Everything in our current handbag has to be transferred into a bag that picks up the dominant color of whatever we're wearing. Some handbags are not large enough to accommodate the wallet we are using, and this means our credit cards and driver's license have to be transferred. A new lipstick might have to be selected to touch up our mouth during the day.

At this point we have to revisit the mirror because, after performing all of the above steps, there is a distinct possibility that our nose has become shiny and we have to reapply a dusting of powder.

Now, we are almost out of the door, if we could just find our keys. After locating them in yesterday's handbag, we only need to find our sunglasses and, yes, we are ready to go.

Wait, we forgot our perfume. Now we're ready — we just have to go to the bathroom.

Now the phone is ringing. We'll just get that. Wrong number.

Which reminds me, where is the cell phone? It's charging in the kitchen.

Wait one second. The dry cleaning tickets are somewhere.

We're out the door. It's just that easy.

We just have to go back in and grab a drink of water.

Bye-bye.

So the next time a man asks you why it takes you so long to get ready, have him read this while he's waiting. Maybe he will understand a little better what goes into being a woman on a daily basis. It is as challenging for us as it is annoying for them. We need steady hands, excellent vision, and an unerring sense of color.

It's different for men. You have one thing. You have a belt . . . and you still miss a loop.

THINGS THAT PALPABLY DON'T WORK

1. Those buttons you push when you stand on a street corner that supposedly trigger the traffic lights.
2. Golf lessons.
3. Wrinkle cream.
4. Estimates.
5. Rat poison.

PLEASE DON'T BE
MY NEIGHBOR

If there is one thing I've learned in my fifty-plus years on the punishing planet we call earth, it's that before buying a property, an inspection of more than just the bricks and mortar of the establishment is essential. When we purchased our first house in Los Angeles, we researched how the house had been built, we conducted a termite test, we obtained a geological report, and we commissioned a land survey. The only thing we forgot to inspect were our neighbors.

The first few nights spent in our new house were relatively peaceful. In retrospect, I think we were so exhausted from unpacking incorrectly labeled boxes we could have slept through a lightning storm at a Metallica concert.

"I love living in the hills," I remember saying to my husband. "At night, I can hear the wind rushing through the trees."

That noise eventually turned out to be the

man across the street trying to start his car.

After a week of interrupted sleep, I decided to enlist the help of my espresso machine and stayed up to discover exactly what was occurring. At 3:00 a.m., I peered out of the window and witnessed a large man wearing a blond wig, ripped T-shirt, and baggy jeans stumbling drunkenly out of his front door and into a dilapidated Cadillac. The man proceeded to repeatedly rev the car's engine for about forty minutes. After revving, he sat in the vehicle and stared into space for a few minutes. Then he proceeded to rev again. Slowly the revver left his car and returned to his house.

"Why didn't you just close the window and buy a white-noise machine?" I can hear you asking me through these pages.

Well, it wasn't that easy. Our bedroom window faced the road. The house had no air-conditioning, so leaving our window open was a necessity. Furthermore, as I see it, white-noise machines only make things noisier. That's why they're called *noise* machines. A quiet machine would only allow the noise in, so just stop your nonsense or I'll get stroppy.

The next day, instead of confronting the bewigged, drunk, large man, I instead decided to approach his elderly, bewigged, drunk, large mother about the nightly disruption.

"Jimmy's eccentric, there's no doubt about it," she confessed as she sloppily watered her flower box. "He's just got home from prison and he likes to drink beer and start up his car and sit in it at night. I'm just glad he don't go nowhere and get into no fights."

"It wakes us up every night. Do you think you could ask him not to do it? Or at least do it earlier in the evening?"

"If it bothers you," she replied, "why don't you move somewhere else, you skinny-assed whore bitch?"

I went in search of a quiet white-noise machine.

Thankfully, it was only a matter of time before the ex-convict was again a convict. I don't know what he did, but I heard some strange noises coming from his house the night he was arrested. I hope it involved a cat and not his mother. The only neighbors then left to concern us were the man next door, whose hobby was hauling cars from a junkyard and restoring them in his driveway, and the French photographer, who photographed nude models on his front lawn. My husband wasn't that concerned about the French photographer.

We exercised more caution when buying our next house. It was located near the top of a peaceful mountain road. On one side was a vacant lot so steep it was impossible to build on and on the other was an older couple with grown children and a cat. We were busy luxuriating in the swimming pool I had always dreamed of owning when an angry woman opened the gate to our backyard.

"The steps to your pool are on my land," she claimed.

"What?" I replied, removing my goggles.

"You heard me. The steps to your pool are on my land."

She handed me a letter from her lawyer demanding we remove the steps that ran down the side of our house to our pool.

We later discovered that land surveys in the hills are not always entirely accurate. The lot next door to us was indeed vacant, but between our house and the vacant lot there was a three-foot easement for a water pipe that fed the house that was positioned immediately below us. That house belonged to the angry woman. The steps in question provided the only access for our pool service and our gardener to enter our backyard. Without them, they would have to lug a lawn mower and pool cleaning equipment into our living room, down our stairs, through our den, and out into the garden.

This was ridiculous. The woman would have to listen to reason. This was Beverly Hills, not the Wild West. My husband arranged a face-to-face meeting with the harridan who was in love with her water pipe. We presented our commonsense case to her, and she presented us with her land survey that showed three stairs indeed extended almost half a foot onto her water pipe easement. She also indicated that there was a distinct possibility that the corner of our pool infringed by a few inches and therefore would have to be removed.

When she left, not only was I angry, I was panicked. My husband was calm.

"She wants money. We'll pay her off and she'll go away."

We contacted her lawyer.

"She's a nightmare," her lawyer explained. "She doesn't want money. She wants her few inches of land. She's a crazy woman. Move your steps. She'll never go away."

"But the steps aren't anywhere near her water pipe. It's a three-foot strip of land that runs down a mountain. It's not a vacation spot," I pleaded.

"She'll never go away," he repeated. "I know. I'm married to her."

There is nothing more dangerous than a litigious person married to a lawyer. Such an individual has nothing to lose and everything to gain. Her lawyer was free and she was sleeping with him. The only thing more difficult than getting our expensive lawyer on the phone was getting him off it. He charged by the sentence. Three years and a six-figure legal bill later, we had twenty-five innocent cement steps destroyed so we could reposition three of them four and a half inches farther toward Mexico. The good news was we had obtained a survey that proved the corner of our pool was indeed on our land, and on this issue at least I got to tell her to shove it.

By this time, the quiet couple next door had moved. It turned out they were only renting the house and the actual owner of the property was eager to lease it again speedily so as not to lose a month's rent. This meant he was not too fussy about the character of prospective renters. Now, I forgot to mention that our house and the house next door were originally one lot. Our house was numbered 225 and the house next door was 225 1/2. This meant that people were constantly ringing our doorbell by mistake. I was now answering my door to a parade of strange women who showed up late at night and asked for Romeo. More important, the new tenant once stole my pizza when it was left on my front stoop. He did. I saw him.

After he left, things got bad. A then-rising starlet, who shall be nameless but not bottomless, moved next door with a husband who had a fierce temper and two vicious hellhounds that frothed at the mouth and spewed saliva through the fence at passersby. Eventually, the lovebirds were divorced and the Irreconcilable Differences moving company appeared one blessed morning. A pink moving truck and a blue moving truck parked outside the house and their possessions were carried out and divided accordingly. She took the furniture, he took the dogs.

Of course, immediately before we moved to Las Vegas, a charming couple bought 225 1/2. For a blissful two weeks we lived side by side in felicitous peace and harmony. Then we moved.

Now we live in an apartment and have no problem with the people who live above us, below us, and next door to us. However, I come in late at night and my dog barks the moment I put my key in the door. They have registered complaints about me.

I have no talent for growing plants. I always kill them. I went into a nursery once and saw my face on a wanted poster.

Vacations of the
Not So Rich and
Famous

There are a few places I want to visit before I die. This is one of the places I visited that almost killed me. I blame Katie Couric and Matt Lauer for this particular experience. They know nothing about it, but still, it's their fault. The *Today* show was being broadcast from France one week. I'm not even sure how I saw the program, because this was before my dog was fifteen and needed to be walked at 6:00 a.m. and before I had a child who had to get to school by eight, so I don't know what I was doing awake at seven in the morning, but I was. This particular morning Katie and Matt were in the Loire Valley. French wine country could not have looked more beautiful. The markets, the vineyards, the castles . . . it was all out of a fairy tale, and I love a fairy tale.

A few weeks later I received the call.

"Hi, this is Andrea, I'm a booker from

Vacations of the Rich and Famous, and we'd like to know if you and your husband would like to go on an all-expenses-paid vacation to the Loire Valley. First-class tickets and accommodations are taken care of. You will be whisked from the airport to your five-star hotel and an unobtrusive film crew will follow you while you sightsee and dine in fabulous restaurants."

I said yes very quickly just in case Andrea had dialed the wrong number and meant to ask someone who was more famous.

The day before we were set to leave for Paris, our itinerary arrived. Martin, who is a much more detail-oriented person than I am, scrutinized the first-class tickets.

"Rita, something is wrong here. It shouldn't take twenty hours to get to Paris."

I looked at the tickets. "Well, we have a two-hour layover in Houston and a six-hour layover in Miami. And we're flying via Canada. I'll call my friend Andrea. There's been a mistake."

There was no mistake. The tickets were indeed first-class, but they had been purchased with frequent-flyer miles and these were the only flights available. The hotel and restaurants had already been reserved and the film crew was on its way from Germany.

"I assure you," my friend Andrea promised, "once you arrive in Paris you'll be whisked to the hotel and from then on everything will be perfect."

I felt better as I thought about how much fun being whisked would be.

"Even though your tickets don't allow it, I'll arrange for you to be let into the first-class lounges on your layovers. Bye," she said, hanging up the phone just a little too quickly.

I swallowed the fact we were not allowed in the first-class lounge in Houston, but I fought our way into the first-class lounge in Miami. They knew nothing about any special arrangements, but a six-hour layover plus a delayed flight added a note of urgency to my plea. I just kept remembering that all we had to do was arrive in Paris and everything would be fantastic.

Twenty-five hours after leaving Los Angeles, we arrived in France. As we waited for our luggage to arrive I scoured the baggage claim area to locate the people who'd be doing the whisking.

A scowling middle-aged man approached.

"Bonjour. I am François. I am your tour guide. *Merde!"* he shrieked. "That is all *your* luggage?"

"Yes. Martin and I have two suitcases

each. If we're filming for five days, we have to wear different clothes."

"This will not fit in my car. You will have to take a train."

"How do I get to a train with all this luggage?"

"That is your problem."

So much for being whisked. We held firm and insisted François drive us to the Loire. We watched as he removed the roof from his convertible and shoved the luggage into the backseat and trunk while mumbling things in French we were thankful we didn't understand. I don't know why someone would meet travelers at the airport in a compact convertible, but there would be many more things I didn't understand to come.

We checked into a lovely hotel that was carved out of limestone two hundred years ago and decorated at about the same time. Martin and I went to sleep for a few hours while the film crew set up breakfast to be filmed on the front lawn. Orange juice, croissants, and eggs waited for us on a small table. They were covered with a plastic sheet to protect them from the rain that was beginning to fall quite heavily.

"You vill sit here and eat zer brekfest like it is not raining," Eva, the German film director, commanded. Martin and I smiled and ate obediently. I like my orange juice watered down anyway, and Martin always enjoys a soggy croissant.

The weather bucked up and our next stop was a busy outdoor market. Parking was a problem for most of the market's visitors, but not for François. François created his own parking spaces. This particular one had the car perched on an island in the middle of a street.

"Is this legal?" I worried.

"*Bien sûr.* It is fine," he said, waving the film crew's van over to park behind us.

Now this was the experience Katie and Matt had promised me. The fruits, cheeses, smells, and sounds of the outdoor market were extraordinary. We arrived back at the car just in time to witness the policeman placing the tickets on the windshields of both vehicles.

François pulled them off and stuffed them in his pocket nonchalantly. We returned back to our prehistoric hotel to rest.

"I will pick you up at five o'clock. Make sure you go to the bathroom before we leave. There are no facilities in the *cave,*" François warned.

"The cave?" I repeated.

"Yes, you are so lucky. Tonight we are having dinner with my friends in a *cave* in wine country."

I wasn't sure how to dress for a cave with no bathroom . . . maybe a burlap dress and astronaut diapers?

We met François's friend André and toured his lush vineyard with the Nazi camera crew trailing behind. Then it was time to enter the cave. Martin and I followed François and André into André's subterranean wine cellar. I know it must be hard to find good cave cleaners these days, but this one really could have used a good dusting. The walls were covered with what I call fungus and what André called mushrooms. He stuck his hand into a cobwebbed wall, pulled out a fungus-covered bottle of wine we would be having with our meal, and wiped it on his pants.

"Fantastique!" he exclaimed Frenchly.

Martin and I sat down with around twenty people and our film crew and ate a menu of varied, unnamed barbecued meats accompanied by fabulous wine. Around ten we all began wandering out of the cave to either find a bathroom or to create one of our own.

The next day's highlight was a trip to a sixteenth-century château. As usual, François created his own parking space between two elm trees and gestured to the film van to park alongside.

"Do you have zer permit?" Eva asked François.

"Pardon?" he replied.

"Did you call ahead and get permission from zer authorities to film in zer castle?" Eva repeated.

"I will do that right now," François replied. "You go on. I will catch up with you."

We were filming outside in the castle gardens when we were stopped by security.

"May I see your film permit?" the guard asked.

"We're with the TV program *Vacations of the Scattered and Disorganized,*" I replied. "Our guide is arriving with it momentarily."

François arrived permitless and entered into a heated argument with the security guard that culminated in money changing hands and our group being able to film anywhere we wanted. When we were done, we returned to our parking spots. We had a parking ticket. There was no parking ticket on the film crew's windshield because there was no windshield. The van had been broken into and all the film crew's passports and wallets had been stolen along with their spare equipment. We returned back to the hotel while the German crew visited the police station.

Our filming temporarily curtailed, we visited François's parents and the school he'd attended as a young boy. No trip to the Loire is complete without these two fascinating stops. When the film crew returned, we visited a small family bakery, an impressionist art museum, and a restaurant situated in a house on a lake. François accrued at least ten more parking tickets.

The final night we all dined together at the limestone hotel and were one big, happy, dysfunctional family. I had one more disagreement with François when he wanted us to take the train back to the airport. We refused, stuffed our luggage back into his convertible, and began our journey back to Los Angeles. This flight was much better. It only took twenty-three hours.

Martin and I still remember our trip to the Loire Valley fondly, and if we ever go back, we're going to look up François. He won't be hard to find . . . I'm pretty sure he's in parking ticket prison.

I have a girlfriend who's so into recycling, she'll only marry a man who's been married before.

WHAT TO WEAR . . . NOT

"Who do you think is crazier, Dolce or Gabbana?" I asked my friend Lisa as I leafed though a fashion magazine.

"Let me see what they've done now," she replied, grabbing the thick, shiny fashion bible from my clutches. "Oh, my God! Why is she naked and bound in electrical wire?"

"It's not electrical wire. It's a pashmina string shawl. Evidently, we're all going to be bound in them by Christmas."

I retrieved my magazine and continued to flip.

"Karl Lagerfeld has been taking his bad dreams a little too seriously as well."

Lisa grabbed the magazine once again.

"She's on fire. Are we all going to have to set ourselves on fire this winter?"

"That's one way to keep warm."

I continued my quest to find a picture of something I would actually wear.

"Oh, now *this* is me. I can see me going to

the bank in this. They might give me some extra money if I agree never to come in again."

"That is scary," Lisa commented, scrutinizing the photograph. "Where are you going to get the gold paint, the feathers, and the pacifier?"

"I don't know. Saks?"

As far as I can see, there is a complete disconnect between the photos in the sleek fashion magazines and the clothes that people actually wear. The models — or, as I like to call them, TPWHs (that's an acronym for telephone poles with hair) — either are starved from birth or have metabolisms like hummingbirds. In any case, they're bonier than fish carcasses.

I can hear the photo editors now: "Push the envelope, Helmut. I've seen the girl in the bikini riding a llama in Marlo Thomas's living room a million times. We want something different."

Not only are the photos different, they are becoming increasingly sexual. I was leafing through a copy of *Vogue* on an airplane and the man next to me became transfixed.

"I have to know. What part of a woman's body is that?" he asked.

"I'm hoping it's her tonsils," I replied, hastily turning the page.

Comfort and time management are really not factors here, I thought as I looked at the woman wearing a pair of shoes that laced to her crotch. *And look at those high heels. The last thing that girl needs is to be taller. If she were a firefighter, she could rescue people without using a ladder.*

"When would a woman actually wear shoes like that?" my puzzled neighbor asked.

"I honestly don't know," I replied. "Maybe in a foot bondage competition."

"Is this the price here?" he inquired.

I leaned over and squinted.

"Yes, they're seven thousand dollars. If it's any consolation, that's for both of them."

Instead of voicing dissent about the too-high cost of too-high heels, not only are women buying these shoes, they're having their feet surgically altered to accommodate them.

I've recently learned that as women age the pads on the balls of their feet thin. There is now an operation that is becoming increasingly more popular: silicone foot implants. I swear I didn't make it up. I saw it on an interview with a surgeon on the Discovery Channel.

"It makes sense," he said. "Women want to look glamorous and this cushions the ball of the foot and keeps it bouncy. It gives the woman a younger foot."

I knew the rest of me was too old, but I was fairly confident about the balls of my feet.

The man handed the magazine back to me.

"You women, you'll buy anything," he said.

He was partially correct. I will and I do, but I rarely buy any outfits I see in the fashion magazines.

I did once spot in a Chanel advertisement an evening gown that I thought would be fun to wear onstage. It was light pink and had a flared skirt dotted with bits of material that were so fine they appeared to be floating. I found the gown on Chanel's Web site. It was haute couture and cost $35,000. I decided it would not be wise for me to have that much fun.

I was coming to the end of the June issue when I spied a pants suit that I coveted. It was made of off-white wool and the trousers flared slightly but not ridiculously at the bottom. The jacket was cut low enough in the front to reveal some bosom, but not an amount that I would consider inappropriate. It appeared not only stylish but comfortable.

"Lisa, look at this. Something I would

actually wear."

Lisa glanced over at the magazine.

"They're not selling the pants suit. It's an ad for that vitamin for women who are pre-menopausal."

"Oh," I said, closing the magazine. "My streak remains intact."

THINGS I NEVER THOUGHT I WOULD SEE IN MY LIFETIME

1. A five-dollar cup of coffee.
2. Television commercials for erectile dysfunction.
3. Paul McCartney getting divorced.
4. A vice president shooting his best friend.
5. A ninety-year-old woman having to take her shoes off in order to put them through the X-ray machine at the airport security checkpoint to ensure they weren't going to explode.

TELEVISION ENVY

It has come to my attention that through the years, in order to entice the public to keep on buying, companies have to make their products either bigger or smaller. The phones, for example, are now so small we can't find them, and the televisions are now so large we need to create special rooms for them.

Forget penis envy and remember television envy. Every man has a friend who has a television that is bigger than his and he wants it. It is not, however, the simple purchasing of an enormous television that can make a man feel complete. The sound system, the blackout curtains, the theater seating, and the acoustic wall panels have to make all of his friends sick with jealousy for a man to really be happy.

When we moved into our new apartment in Las Vegas, my husband and I came to the agreement that I could have a lavender bedroom if he could have his own, very special, macho television room. The family den, which used to be a comfortable environment where children could play and people could eat, talk, and laugh, has now morphed into what is now commonly referred to as a "home theater" — a place that must remain as dark as a well and as quiet as a morgue.

Since we were moving to a new town and since we don't like to reject anybody and since he came in with a very low quote, we went with the first person we interviewed to build my husband's fantasy room. The media man was just starting his own company and his eyes contained a sadness that indicated he needed us. He also had a soft voice and a gentleness about him that prevented us from suing him.

My husband and It'sNotMyFault (as I shall call him) decided on a front-projection screen that was so wide it failed to go through the door that led into the room. Rather than compromise on the size of the screen, a new door was created and the old one was paneled over. It'sNotMyFault also made the decision to hire a family member to cover the walls with a special material that both absorbed and ricocheted sound at the same time. I don't know how this man (whom I shall call IDidn'tDoIt) would know very much about material given that he had never owned a shirt with sleeves and most of his body was kept warm by tattoos. He was also put in charge of the all-important blackout curtains, intended to keep sunlight away from the screen. This task seemed as imperative as that of a bodyguard assigned to keep young boys away from a king's pretty daughter.

"Are you sure these blackout curtains will make it dark enough in here?" my husband inquired worriedly. "Maybe you should double-line them? I don't want any light shining on my projection screen. It's very sensitive. A mark can appear on it even if you just speak badly about it."

"I guarantee you, no light will make it through these curtains. Your screen is safe. I have these very same curtains in my home and they work perfectly in my home theater."

It struck me as odd that a man who couldn't afford a shirt would be able to spring for a home theater, but I guess many men would now rather be homeless than home-theater-less. Anyway, he was right about the curtains. The minute he put them up, I tripped over everything in the room. It is so dark in there that while trying to eat a sandwich I actually missed my mouth. I pointed out to my husband that even real movie theaters have some lights in them so you can see an aisle or an exit. He said it compromised the whole experience and that was exactly why he was creating his own home theater.

I became even more suspicious of It'sNotMyFault when none of the equipment he arrived with came with instructions, bills, warranties, or even boxes. The DVD player, VCR, CD player, and receiver were all top-of-the-line, It'sNot boasted.

"What do we do if it breaks?" I asked.

"Call me and I'll . . . find . . . I mean, I'll buy you a new one."

It'sNot was a man of his word. Within the first six months nearly every component proved to be defective, and within weeks he arrived with an unwrapped, semi-new one.

"It's not my fault," It'sNot would say. "My supplier is letting me down."

What is even more likely is that his "supplier" couldn't find him. It'sNot's home phone had been disconnected and he was now reachable only by a cell phone that he refused to answer. When we left a message the call was always returned within the month and a creative excuse was concocted to explain the delay.

"I lost it." "Someone stole it." "I was in the hospital getting a knee replacement." That last one was my personal favorite. That took imagination.

No mechanical gadget was overlooked in my husband's playroom.

"Why do we need a remote control for the curtains?" I asked. "We can just pull them closed. It's not like we can't reach them. I can simply walk to the window, the same way I do in every other room in the house."

"It's all in," my husband explained. "We might as well get everything. It was included in the quote."

The personal remote control box that activated the DVD player, VCR, CD player, curtains, and TV is in fact a triumph. It is so simple even a child can use it and so heavy only a professional wrestler can lift it. It also has to be left on the charger at all times or else it will run out of juice and have to be reprogrammed.

I have not yet begun to talk about speakers. Since we were building the room from scratch, the speakers were to be inserted into the wall. They would be as inconspicuous as they would be powerful. They would also be spaced unevenly the first time. The subsequent redrilling took place after the ultra-sensitive projection screen had been assembled. A mysterious scratch appeared on the screen, caused by either It'sNot or IDidn't. We could never determine which one was the culprit. I only know it wasn't their able assistant, INeverShowUp.

We disagreed on the seating. My husband wanted theater chairs that reclined, but because the door had been repositioned due to the size of the screen, large chairs that weren't flush against the back wall would have made it challenging for even a gymnast to enter the room. So we decided on a large sofa that my husband is dissatisfied with to this day.

While the rest of our fairly large apartment took about six months to finish, this smallest room in the house took over a year. The wall covering needed special glue. IDidn't chose to apply this glue on our balcony, leaving a stain that says a big hello to me whenever I slide open the door.

"It will disappear over time," IDidn't promised, neglecting to indicate which generation would finally walk out onto our balcony and not say, "What the hell is this?"

In the end, was it worth it? My husband says yes, and reluctantly I agree with him. The screen is fantastic, the sound is crisp, and when we rent a DVD it is a luxury to be able to sit in our own home theater and say, "Boy, this is a crappy movie."

I was a boring kid. Whenever we played doctor, the other children always made me the anesthesiologist.

THE ABBREVIATION GENERATION

One of the many technological innovations I didn't see coming was texting. I was introduced to texting by Lindsay, my friend's fourteen-year-old daughter. I didn't know what she had to say to her friend that was so important, but there she was, in the corner by herself, typing madly into her phone. I sauntered over to try to understand.

"What does 'LOL' mean?" I asked, looking over her shoulder.

"Laugh out loud," Lindsay replied with barely concealed derision.

"Makes sense. So I guess 'cn u c me 2nite?' means 'Can you see me tonight?' "

"Yes." She sighed.

I peered over her shoulder as she attempted to turn away, and caught a glimpse of her friend's response: "Cnt w8t 2 c u 2."

Lindsay typed, "Cnt tlk nw."

" 'Can't talk now.' Why can't you talk

now?" I asked.

"Because you're looking over my shoulder," Lindsay said, stuffing her phone in her handbag.

"I c," I said, taking the hint and sauntering back whence I'd come.

IM, or instant messaging, is for me the most irritating of the new forms of meaningless communication. I'll be typing a vital e-mail and suddenly something not authored by me will appear on the screen. In a way, IM is a kind of schoolyard power play: *stop doing whatever you're doing and play with me.*

"Hi, Rta, whssup?" popped up on my computer screen a few days ago. Lindsay, who didn't want to talk to me at all when I was actually in the room with her, now wanted to have a casual conversation with me when I was across town and busy doing something else.

"Bsy," I replied, using my new form of vowel-less verbiage.

I guess Lndsy was offended by my lack of response because she hasn't IM'd me lately.

The abbreviation that makes the least sense to me these days is "Have a good one." Logically, the meaning of "Have a good one" is "Have a good day." *Day* and *one* not only have the same number of letters, they each have one syllable. Where are we saving time here?

Whatever is another popular contemporary expression. It is all-encompassing and yet noncommittal at the same time.

"I hate you."

"Whatever."

"I love you."

"Whatever."

"I'm leaving you."

"Have a good one."

But even this one word isn't brief enough. *Whatever* has now itself been distilled to my new favorite abbreviation: *evs.*

Evs exhibits a disaffected ennui that demonstrates you can't even be bothered to form the three syllables that would convey your disinterest. You're on top of things, and no matter what occurs you will survive.

It doesn't stop there. Abbreviations are now being reduced to symbols. I always thought *on* and *off* were two of the briefest yet most efficient words in the English language. What have they done that is so wrong that they can't live on my phone anymore? As I stare at the keyboard of my new cell phone, it appears to me that those simple words have been replaced by a shoe and a feather. If I want to make a call, I don't know whether to press *stomp* or *tickle.*

So I have concluded today's generation has become so sophisticated in the age of too much communication that we now have no need to use words and we're gradually reverting back to hieroglyphics.

Evs. ∼*−∧.

My grandmother was a very tough cookie. She buried three husbands. Two of them were just napping.

THE ADVANTAGE OF VINTAGE

Attending a party the other night, I looked down at what I was wearing and thought, *You know you're getting older when you're wearing vintage Chanel and you're the original owner.* I remembered buying this ridiculously expensive outfit twelve years ago and thinking I was crazy, but amortized through the years it had turned out to be a good investment.

At the time, I'd told my husband that it was a good investment, and he said, "An investment is when you put money into something and when you take it out you have more money."

I'd replied, "An investment is also when you put money into something and when you go to take it out there's nothing there. We've made a lot of those investments. At least I can wear this one."

It's true that good clothes last forever. It's also true that cheap ones last a long time too. For instance, I have T-shirts I can't throw away because they're good for when I condition my hair. I also have stockings with holes in them that I can wear under slacks. You get the idea. One of the harsh facts of life is that as you get older, your wardrobe expands and your closet seems smaller. I've had to begin piling sweaters on top of shelves that NBA players couldn't reach. I'm not the only one with this problem; I read that Cher bought the house next door to hers and converted it into a closet. I don't know how long I'm going to live, but I'm saving up my money in case I have to buy the house next door.

One of the pluses of age is that things you have owned in the past come back into style. I've learned the hard way never to discard any article of clothing in my closet. One of my few regrets in life is a leopard jacket (fake; don't get mad at me) that I gave to a friend of mine. Leopard was so over that year. I was absolutely sure that the only time anyone would ever see that print again was at the zoo. In fact, leopard was so passé, I felt the actual animal might even be eliminated from the feline exhibition. That was a mere five years ago, and this year leopards are everywhere. They're on feet, hands, waists, heads, handbags, and most of all my friend's torso. She still wears my jacket, and every time I see her pairing it with black slacks and looking chic, I want it back.

I did, however, learn my lesson. I'd thought peasant skirts had seen the end of their life expectancy, but last year they were more ubiquitous than pigeons in a park. I was ready. There was a store that I used to frequent when I lived in New York twenty years ago that constructed long flowing skirts out of antique fabrics. Being a big believer in covering my legs and not wanting to wear jeans every single day, I bought three of them: a black lace one, an apricot organza one, and a navy velvet one. I've moved many times, and each time I've looked at the skirts I thought it was time to separate from them but couldn't. They've joined me in seven different houses. For twenty years I've seen them peeking at me from the back of each closet. I could almost hear them saying, *Is it time for me again yet? Am I going out today?* and, sometimes sadly, *Why don't you love me anymore? What did I do that was so wrong?*

I am proud to say that this year, I've worn two of them, the black one and the blue one. I updated them slightly by adding a few chain belts. I'd already owned the belts but had worn them separately. I put four together and all of a sudden they were trendy. Each time I've ventured out wearing one of my antique skirts, young women have come up to me and asked me where I bought it. I tell them, "I bought it in a store in New York that no longer exists. I carted it around with me through seven different houses. I waited patiently for twenty years, and at the right moment I paired it with some tarnished belts and, voilà, it's something you want. You can't have it. You're not vintage."

I was happily providing housing for clothes I might never again touch when I got a notice in my mailbox from a resale store. It said, "Are you wasting closet space on things you no longer wear? Bring your clothes to me and I'll sell them for you. I'm Susie the Spacemaker." There was even a handwritten P. S. on the bottom that said, "Rita, I have lots of customers your size." I couldn't tell if it was real or if it was computer-printed (marketers are so adept at writing lies on junk mail these days), but I realized it could be a sign that the universe was telling me to let go, and so I made the trek to visit Susie.

The neighborhood was a little dicey. Susie was located in between a massage parlor and a cheap motel. I rang the doorbell. I was scrutinized and eventually buzzed in. The place smelled like old wool. Women were busily holding dated clothing up to themselves in front of mirrors and then disappearing into the changing booths.

"I'll be with you in a minute," said the frazzled saleswoman working the cash register. "There," she said to the customer, wrapping up a coat, a pants suit, and an evening dress. "All that, and for only sixty dollars."

"Thank you, Susie."

"No, thank *you,* Stacey. See you again soon."

I was jealous. There were women out there who weren't like Cher and me. There were women out there who could let go of their clothes and let other people enjoy them. There were women out there who had room in their closets for new purchases and who didn't have to pile them to Pluto.

"That *is* a good deal," I said to Stacey, admiring her purchases. "I love that coat — I love the collar and I love the shape. And I saw you try it on. It fits you perfectly."

"I know," Stacey said. "It's mine. I'm buying it back."

Evidently, Cher and I have company.

These days it seems everybody has a tattoo. I would never get one, but luckily, on my left leg, I have a vein in the shape of a ship.

THE PROOF IS IN THE CHILD

Becoming a mother late in life did not prevent me from worrying about absolutely everything that occurred in the course of our child's development.

Although our daughter is, of course, a genius, she was not an early crawler. She was, however, an early roller. At seven months, she had mastered the roll so thoroughly there was no need for her to crawl. She could roll wherever she wanted to. I would hold her bottle across the room and she would roll to it. I would tempt her with her favorite bunny and she would roll to it. I pictured her wedding: the guests waiting, the groom watching, and my daughter rolling down the aisle.

Children develop different skills at different times, the child-rearing encyclopedia explained. *Don't worry if your child isn't doing the same things as other children.*

I repeated that mantra in my mind as I

watched my baby propel herself across the room like a drunk while my friend Sheri's little boy, who was the same age, crawled around the room quicker than a crab on crack.

"Her bottom has to be up in the air," Sheri told me. "If you get her bottom up in the air, everything else follows naturally."

I would lift Molly's bottom up in the air and say, "Hand, hand, foot, foot." Instead of moving forward, when I let her go she would collapse on the rug and, of course, roll to her chosen destination. I decided to let my child move diagonally until it occurred to her that there were easier ways to travel.

At about eight and a half months, Molly created a kind of soldier-shimmy across the floor as if she were avoiding enemy fire. It would take her approximately ten minutes to travel two feet. The good news was she had stopped rolling, and the better news was she was now very slowly cleaning our floors. As her shimmy became more and more adept I became confident that the army was in her future.

Molly began to crawl at ten months. It was only then that I realized the joy of having a baby that didn't yet crawl. All those blessed times when I could leave her in one place, turn my head for an instant, and expect her to be in roughly the same place when I turned back were over. Now, although not a crab on crack, she was certainly a turtle on speed. Of course, by now Sheri's little boy was already standing.

"You need a portable playpen," Sheri advised. "Clayton loves it. That's how he learned how to stand. He pulls himself around in a circle all day, and boy, does he get tired."

That sounded good to me, especially since at night I performed my live stage show and at Molly's nap time I attempted to write this book. We ordered a playpen with a disco. It included a musical chicken as well as balls the baby could prod and pound. My husband fastened the hinges of the playpen/disco together and we waited for the magic to happen. Very quickly Molly discovered the musical chicken. I've never heard "Old McDonald" played in a disco, but then I don't get out much.

Instead of supporting herself and moving around the playpen and learning to stand, Molly decided that the playpen was a movable environment. She used her head to push the playpen to wherever she wanted to be.

It was another month before Molly could

stand and make her way around the playpen like a baby inmate looking at freedom over a colored plastic wall. Of course, by now, Sheri's little boy was walking.

"You mean you don't have a walker?" Sheri asked incredulously. "That's how Clayton learned. You sit them in the middle and they wheel themselves around. It's great. You don't have to carry them around all the time and they develop coordination."

The walker was less of a learning device and more of a weapon. Who decided it was wise to give a baby a set of wheels? Every time we turned around, a rolling plastic table sailed into our shins. After a few unfortunate encounters with his tail, our dog took refuge underneath my desk and only came out when the wheeling monster was asleep.

At about thirteen months Molly began to walk. It was actually more of a stagger. She would take a few steps and then, without warning, just tip over like a table that had three legs. Of course, by now Clayton was running.

"Have you childproofed your house yet?" Sheri inquired.

"No, not yet."

"You'd better do it soon," she warned. "Now that Molly's walking she'll be into everything. The other day Clayton opened our liquor cabinet and tried to mix a martini."

The next day, my husband and I drove to our favorite store, Babies Are Expensive, and stocked up on devices designed to prevent babies from harming themselves. We bought:

1. Plastic table-corner covers, none of which fit the dimensions of any of our tables.
2. Locks for our sliding glass doors that already had locks.
3. A lock for our toilet lid to prevent our child from drowning that also prevented me from going to the bathroom.
4. Drawer stoppers that had to be drilled into the wood of our cabinetry.
5. And the only thing we really needed — plastic covers for our electrical outlets, which cost fifty cents.

Molly never attempted to run into a table corner, pry open a glass door, swim in the toilet, stand in a drawer, or mix a margarita, although I did suggest a few of those activities to her so as to justify the holes in our furniture. I suppose it's better to be safe than bloody, but most of the things that were true for Sheri's baby were not true for mine.

Toilet training is next. Sheri says she bought a musical potty that plays a fanfare whenever her child christens it and it has been very effective. I think I'll take her advice and pick one up. Not for Molly, for me. I can't figure out how to unlock my toilet.

I'm kind of a wimp. I was once hospitalized for three weeks with a bad perm.

THE PILLOW SHOW

I can't remember when my fascination with fancy pillows began, but in my fifties it is alive and well and threatening our marriage.

"Rita, it's easier to undress a nun than it is to get into this bed," my husband moans nightly.

When I make our bed, I have a strict and rigid system of pillow placement. Putting the show together is a task that rivals the creation of a Broadway musical, so I will attempt to explain my pillow philosophy. This is not written in stone, by the way. It's just how I've choreographed my own personal pillow show. However, I hope it will help you to create your own unique pillow vision.

1. The two anchor pillows must be leaned diagonally against the headboard. These pillows will never be seen in their entirety, so they don't have to be gorgeous, but

they do have to be attractive enough to keep the integrity of the pillow show intact. They should, although it is not a prerequisite, have ruffles around the edges because although they will never be seen completely until the pillow mountain is moved, an edge might peek out. They must also be large and sturdy. They should be square rather than rectangular to give dimension to the piece. They must be stuffed with foam rather than feathers because they are the foundation of the structure.

2. On top of the anchor pillows are placed the shams. A sham is rectangular, and though not as dense as the anchor pillows, it must still be firm. While an anchor pillow is usually one color, a sham can begin to have a pattern. A sham is bigger than a regular pillow and for some reason is absurdly expensive.

3. With the pillows that lean against the sham, you can begin to go a little crazy. I would suggest two square or squarish textured (possibly velvet) pillows that express your personality. I'm a butterfly and tassel woman myself. I don't know what that says about me. Maybe I wear

too many colors and need a haircut.

4. Next, we're going to change shapes and go for a single round antique pillow that somebody's grandmother would have owned. This is a conversation pillow. Example: "Is that your grandmother's pillow?" "No, but I bought it in an antique store, and the salesman said it may have belonged to Eleanor Roosevelt." This is your important pillow.

5. We're coming to the end now. The bolster or accent pillow is the final bit of foam that you will place on your bed. It should lie on one side of your important pillow and should be placed at an angle so as not to appear studied.

6. You will realize that I have left out pillows that you actually place your head on. These must be kept in a closet and placed on the bed only after the decorative pillows have been removed. They are functional pillows and do not belong in pillow show business.

Again, these are only my suggestions. I leave the actual creation up to you.

My husband's question is, "We are the

only two people who go into the bedroom. Who are we doing the little pillow show for?"

And to tell you the truth, I don't know. I only know that I love my pillows . . . and I have to do the show.

I just bought this new mattress and I can roll on it and not disturb my husband all night. His mattress is in the other room.

THE SCAN

One of the good things about advancing years is discovering new ways to save money while spending it.

"Could you please scan this?" requested my expert shopping friend Joyce as she handed a beaded evening gown across the counter to Freda, the frazzled saleswoman.

"Sure, honey."

"I like it when they call me 'honey,' " Joyce confessed to me. "It makes me feel loved."

"Why did you ask her to scan it? Isn't the price on the label?" I inquired.

"I have a feeling," Joyce announced. "That gown has been marked down three times, from three seventy-five to two ninety-five to two forty-five. It's on the take-fifty-percent-off-ticketed-price rack. This is the Columbus Day sale, which means take off an extra thirty percent. Plus, I have a ten-dollars-off coupon that's good until five o'clock. I could take this shiny little girl home for about seventy-eight bucks."

"Plus tax."

"It's a no-tax day, Rita. Gee, you are such an amateur."

"I have another stupid question."

"What now?" Joyce asked in a voice laced with condescension.

"The tag says it's a size fourteen. You're a four."

"I know. What's your point?"

"You can't wear it, pencil legs," I replied, getting even with her for the "amateur" comment.

"I don't want to wear it," she admitted. "I don't even want to buy it. I just want to know what I could have bought it for if I wanted it and had they had it in my size."

"I see," I said, not seeing.

Freda had been strangely quiet during our conversation. As she glanced up from the computer, Joyce and I both tried to look her in the eye. She looked away.

"She's hiding something," Joyce whispered to me.

Freda leaned across the computer, crushing her ample bosom against the screen. "Baby doll, come closer."

Joyce met her halfway across the counter.

"Eight dollars and fifty cents."

"What?" Joyce whispered.

"What is it?" I asked. "Is it not on sale after all? Did someone put it on the wrong rack? I hate that. The people who do that should be punished. They have no idea of the hardship they cause."

"Rita, shut up," Joyce snapped. "This is serious."

Freda lowered both her head and her voice.

"Someone has made a mistake and put the wrong price in the computer," she confessed. "It's in the computer, cutie pie. Once it's in the computer, Bill Gates couldn't get it out."

"Will anyone get fired if I buy this gown for this price?" Joyce asked. "I don't really care, but I'd just like to know."

"No one will suffer. It will go down in the books the same as any other sale. If you don't buy it, sugarplum, I will."

"What mistake? Who's going to get fired?" I demanded. "I can't be your friend anymore unless you tell me immediately."

Joyce looked around before whispering hoarsely to me, "An error had been made. If I act quickly, I can purchase a beaded gown that was originally three hundred and seventy-five dollars for eight dollars and fifty cents."

"Oh, my God!" I said, clutching my chest. "Is that legal?"

"It's not only legal, it's meant to be. The shopping gods are looking down on me. It's a bargain triumph."

"But it's a size fourteen."

"I'm not taking you with me anymore, Rita. You're a real consumer pessimist."

Freda became impatient. "I've got other customers, ladies. What's it going to be?"

"It's getting hot in here," Joyce mumbled in my direction. "Freda's not calling me endearing names anymore. She wants the dress."

"She would. She looks to me like she's a size fourteen."

"I can't let that sway me. I was here first. I was the one who asked her to scan it. It's rightfully mine."

"You're a machine."

"I'll take it," Joyce announced, sifting through her overstuffed purse and emerging with her credit card.

"It's eight dollars and fifty cents. Why don't you pay cash?" I asked.

"If you pay cash, you only enjoy the shopping win once. This way, when the bill arrives at the end of the month, I can relive it."

"Hung or in the bag?" Freda asked curtly,

not bothering now to address us as people at all.

"Hung."

Joyce turned to me. "Before you ask, if you take it home hung, you get a free hanger."

"I knew that one."

With palpable bad grace, Freda encased the beaded prize in a plastic bag and handed it to Joyce.

"Here."

"Thank you," Joyce replied. "It's for you." She sadly handed the package back to Freda. "I can't wear it," my friend admitted. "I just had to buy it."

"Oh, honeybun, I can't take this," said Freda guiltily. "At least let me give you the money."

"No," Joyce said. "You wear the dress and think of me. Just give me the hanger."

And with that we slunk away in the direction of the escalator.

"You do know you just paid eight dollars and fifty cents for a hanger, don't you?" I asked.

"Yes, Rita, I do. I didn't really want the dress, I only wanted the glory."

"Didn't you mention you have a coupon that entitled you to an extra ten percent off until five o'clock? It's five to five. You could have gotten another eighty-five cents off."

Joyce immediately stopped in her tracks and looked at me with a new respect.

"You've learned well, Rita. We're going back."

I have a new push-up bra. It's an underwire made of this special new metal that's attracted to the fillings in my teeth.

It's My Potty and I'll Cry If I Want To

I promised myself I wouldn't stress out about toilet-training our baby. After all, this is something to which everybody eventually catches on. I've never heard the sentence "Marissa is twenty-seven and she's still in diapers. She just can't quite get the hang of it."

I didn't want to push my daughter into something that she wasn't ready for, but without becoming too graphic, the water-tight seals on the paper panties weren't as reliable as they appeared to be in the commercials. The sooner I could complete the diaper stage the better.

My friends weren't much help when I needed their guidance. Because I'd waited until I was older to become a mother, their children were already in their teens; consequently their memories of child rearing were a little hazy.

"How did you toilet-train Alexandra?" I

asked my friend Marilyn.

"I don't remember," she responded, as did all my other friends.

My father revealed quite a bit about his participation in the messier parts of my infancy when he asked, "What's toilet training?"

My British mother-in-law had the best answer when I asked her about toilet-training my husband.

She said, "He just did it naturally by himself at eighteen months. He was a fastidious child."

I didn't believe her, but after eighteen years of marriage to her son, I knew not to question her.

"You have to wait until they're ready. If you don't, it can cause problems in later life" was the only clue people would give me.

"What kind of problems?" I wondered.

Most children are frightened of monsters and snakes. I'd hate for my child to be frightened of toilets and flushing.

The books I read were also unhelpful.

"Introduce your child to the potty gradually," one book advised. "Buy one early and just casually leave it in the bathroom."

My husband and I ordered a personalized potty when Molly was twenty months old.

Her name appeared on the back of it in red, shiny letters, as if she were the star of the seat.

"Molly, this is your potty," I said, introducing her to her new friend. "Do you like it?"

"Yah," she said.

For some reason, the first words my child uttered all sounded Swedish.

"Do you want to sit on it?"

"Noh."

She then went and found her favorite stuffed toy and placed it with a flourish in the plastic hole in the center of the seat.

"For bunny."

Well, not really, I thought. "Yes, for bunny," I said out loud. I didn't want it to affect her later in life.

We left the potty in the bathroom and it subsequently became home to various stuffed animals. I checked the books and none of them referred to the my-child-thinks-the-potty-is-a-place-to-keep-her-toys syndrome. I didn't mention it; I didn't want it to affect her later in life.

A few months later, Molly and I were playing with dolls in the potty when the phone rang. It was my friend Marilyn.

"I just remembered. We had a musical potty. Every time your child uses it, it plays a little song. Alexandra loved it. It worked like a charm."

I hung up the phone.

"Martin, get the car keys. We're going potty shopping."

We arrived home, assembled the musical potty, and placed it in her bathroom. It had an infrared light positioned under the seat that sensed when the child sat down and would play a musical flourish as if introducing the queen. My mother-in-law would approve of it.

"Martin, I hope she doesn't carry this association with her in later life. What if every time she hears music she loses control of her bladder?"

"Alexandra plays the piano. She doesn't have to wear Depends," my husband reasoned.

"You're right. Molly, come here. I want to show you something."

My child appeared at the door of her bathroom.

"Molly, this is your new potty. It plays music. Do you want to try it?"

"Yah."

She then disappeared into her room and reappeared with her bunny. She placed the bunny in the plastic cup, which sang its little tune. She laughed, sat down on the floor, and played with it for a good hour. I was patient. A few days later, when changing her diaper, I asked her if she wanted to sit on the new potty. We walked into the bathroom and she sat down. It played the musical flourish. She jumped up as if it were on fire and began to cry. Hoping I hadn't affected her negatively for the rest of her life, I went back to the potty drawing board.

One day, while scouring the parenting section of the bookstore, I spotted it: the potty video. I didn't know if this would help, but I knew I couldn't fail more miserably than I had previously. I showed it to Molly, and she liked the photo of the baby on the cover. The animated tape was all about a little girl graduating from diapers. Molly loved it and requested it every day for a month. I could sing "The Potty Song" in my sleep. I was humming it during the day. I think I even sang it by mistake one night in my act. There was one problem. Although we owned a personalized potty and a musical potty, we now needed to find a cheap, plastic, old-fashioned version like the one in the video.

We finally succeeded in tracking one down. Molly sat down on it and, with the video playing in the background, we had our first success. We looked at it. We cheered. We kissed her. We considered saving what was in the potty, but then came to our senses. We prematurely congratulated ourselves about conquering toilet training. It turned out Molly thought she only had to do it once.

In her baby mind, she was thinking, *I'm glad that's over. Now I can go back to my good ol' diapers and they'll leave me alone.*

It took another month but, thanks to the video, she was trained by the time she was two years and two months. My mother-in-law wasn't impressed.

"In England all babies are trained by eighteen months. They do it naturally."

"That's because everything in Britain is better than everything in America," I replied.

"Yes, that's correct."

My friend's going through menopause. Her hot flashes are so severe, she's been banned from Baskin-Robbins.

To Hell in a
Handbag

I'm a law-abiding woman, really. I never thought I was the sort of person who would end up in handbag prison.

I didn't think anyone would ever know. The bag had *Made in France* stamped on its inside and even had the signature lock and key connected to the gold zipper. Anyway, it wasn't my fault. Let me take you back to the days when I roamed the department store aisles freely, and allow me to explain why I feel I'm not guilty.

In the past five years something has gone extremely awry with the handbag industry. Handbags are no longer abused leather sacks that women fill with makeup, money, and lint-covered mints. They are now more valuable than jewelry and rarer than truffles. In the old days, I would see a handbag in a magazine or a store and if I liked it, I would buy it. I would use it for a year or so and then throw it away, thereby avoiding the risk of not being handbag-current. Then one day, everything changed.

I don't know if Louis Vuitton was an actual person, but if he was, I certainly hope he once ordered something that he really wanted and that it never arrived.

But I'm getting ahead of myself. First, I have to deal with the overwhelming feelings of guilt attached to the action of ordering a handbag from a snobby store when there are perfectly acceptable handbags in the world that desperately need owners. I'm not like that. Really. My dog is from a pound, and I only book a manicure if I obviously need one. I just got caught up in LV frenzy. It was the handbag with multiple LVs in all different colors that I lusted after. And, again, it wasn't my fault. It went with everything and it was perfect for spring.

So early one morning, I marched into a self-important luggage store that seemed cleaner than a laboratory where they develop important drugs, approached the pony-tailed, bat-faced woman behind the counter, and squeaked in a voice that sounded like me when I was twelve, "I want to buy a handbag."

"Which one?" the too-young-to-be-that-pinched woman asked in an accent that sounded Japanese-Italian.

251

"This one," I replied.

I opened my purse and began to search for the photo I had ripped out of the magazine. (A magazine I had purchased, by the way, not one from the waiting room of a dentist's office.)

"It's in here somewhere," I explained, emptying many different shades of lipsticks and glosses onto the glass counter.

You see, that's another reason I wanted that particular handbag. I'm constantly searching for a bag that's big enough to hold my essentials, but not so big that it encourages me to include nonessential items in my inner handbag mix, thereby causing me to empty the contents on a counter in order to find the item I'm looking for. I also need straps that are long enough to snuggle my shoulders but not so long that I couldn't slip them over my wrist if my shoulders were already in use. In the picture I was desperately searching for, I had found just that: the perfect handbag.

"I'll come back when you've found it," batwoman announced with a haughtiness that can only be mustered by someone making minimum wage in an incredibly expensive store.

"Here it is." I held up the wrinkled picture of my dream bag.

Batty grabbed the picture, brought it over to a folder, and began to flip through plastic-encased photographs of Louis's creations.

"Hmmm . . . the waiting list for that style is six months to a year, but I'll be happy to take your name and number."

With that, she picked up a tattered notebook, turned to a particularly inky page, and presented it to me.

"Sign here," she commanded.

I gazed at the page filled with desperate women's signatures and noticed the top ones were beginning to fade.

"You know, I could get this handbag sooner than you think. Many of these women could be dead by now."

"I have no way of knowing that until I notify them."

Evidently there is no laughing in the bat cave.

I decided to allow the practical side of my brain to have a voice.

"Is there another style that might be available sooner?"

She actually laughed. I had finally said something funny.

One month later, I received a call from the store saying that a handbag had arrived. It was not the handbag I had ordered, but it

253

was a style that was in demand.

I flew into the shop at 10:01 the next morning only to find that the bag had been purchased by a client who had made the journey the night before. I felt rejected by the woman, the bag, and Louis V. himself. I was neither important enough nor quick enough to cajole this store into accepting my eight hundred dollars plus tax.

Shuffling dejectedly back to my car, I spotted a woman carrying a multicolored LV bag. It was not the one I had ordered, but at this point I was happy to accept a knapsack.

I accosted the unsuspecting woman.

"Where did you get it? Is there another store that had better connections than this one? Did you pay extra? Are you someone special?" I had so many questions.

"It's a fake," she whispered.

I inspected it.

"The reds are not quite the same red," she explained. "That's the only difference."

"I can live with that. Where did you get it?"

"I know a guy who has a handbag store. He gets the best stuff."

"Where is it?" I demanded.

"He moves around. Right now he's look-ing for a new location. Give me your number and I'll call you after he calls me."

Oh, great, I'm on another list, I thought.

I decided to leave it to fate; whichever person called me first would be the one to get my money.

My connection phoned a week later.

"This is Cindy. I met you in the parking lot of the mall," she whispered conspiratorially. "My guy has another place. Two twenty-two West Apache, suite five-oh-two. Tell him Cindy sent you. He might give you a free pair of Dior sunglasses. I send him a lot of people."

I didn't hesitate. Hesitation had cost me my last bag and delivered me into this predicament in the first place. I pulled into the mini-mall and walked to suite 502. It was closed. The blinds were pulled shut and there was no name on the door.

He can't have moved already, I thought. *The woman only called me ten minutes ago.*

I pushed on the door and heard the unmistakable happy chatter of women considering potential purchases.

"I love this one."

"Yes, but this one is even better."

"Buy them both."

I felt a shiver run up my spine, down my arm, and into my current handbag. The deliberately undecorated room was filled with folding tables showcasing many of the different styles of bags that were totally unavailable to customers who walked into stores hoping to buy the bags legitimately. On the walls were makeshift racks where more initialed bags hung like dead meat.

Directly in front of me I saw my dream bag. It was the last one of its kind. I saw another woman look at it. I turned primal and grabbed it off the rack.

"How much is this?" I asked the man who wore a gold chain, sunglasses, and what appeared to be a full wig.

"Fifty dollars, cash."

"I know Cindy."

"Forty, and I'll throw in a pair of sunglasses. Cindy's a good girl."

I wore my fake handbag proudly until the LVs began to fade where they rubbed against my lawbreaking body.

It was Cindy who shopped me (no pun intended). They found her list of co-conspirators and she gave me up along with the rest of her friends in exchange for her own freedom.

I didn't care. I had the handbag I wanted. I paid only forty bucks for it and I'll be out soon. I'd do it again. Cindy, meanwhile, has entered the Handbag Protection Program. She lives somewhere in Iowa and is only allowed to carry her possessions around in a paper bag.

P.S.: I was notified a month after I was released that my dream handbag had arrived. I told the bat-faced woman I didn't want it anymore. It felt good.

I don't want to be in good shape anymore. I don't want to be one of those women who look great from the back and then turn around and frighten people.

Undercover Wear

"This panel holds in your stomach, and this panel slims your thighs," said Lucille, the overweight underwear specialist who had been flown in especially to lecture on the benefits of the new line of body bossers.

She then proceeded to hold up a Lycra garment that appeared big enough to fit a three-year-old.

"Does it stretch?" I asked.

"Yes, but only in certain places. It's a miracle garment."

As I tugged and pleaded with it in the dressing room, I began to believe. It certainly was a miracle garment. It would be a miracle if I could get it on, a miracle if I could walk, and a miracle if I could breathe.

For a while there it seemed we were making progress in recognizing that women could dress, get on with their day, and remove their clothes without incurring red welts. I remember my mother and her girdle dance. I was not yet ten and didn't yet understand the demands placed on a woman's waist.

"Do you need help?" I recall asking her as I witnessed the tops of her legs turning blue.

"No, I'll get it eventually," she puffed.

"Why do you have to wear that thing?"

"Your father and I are going out to dinner tonight. If I don't put this on, I'll never fit into my dress."

"How are you going to eat anything?"

"I'll eat when I get home."

"Then why are you going out to dinner?"

"To prove I can fit into the dress."

As I grew older, I paid very little attention to the role a girdle might play in a woman's life. That was for my mother, not for me. Anyway, I was a dancer and had a stomach that was flatter than a supermodel's chest. Now, after twenty years and a baby (all right, I adopted, but I still think that counts), I was in search of the sort of garment I had ignored for decades, with the additional pressure of it needing to be entirely invisible to the human eye.

I had already been warned about the evils of displaying a panty line by Bonnie, my lingerie-addicted friend.

"Look at you. You have a V in the back. How can you live with yourself?" she asked me in horror.

In Bonnie's defense, she is single and still only wears bra and panty sets. Excuse me, bra and thong sets. She would not be caught dead in panties. The old saying was "What if a car hits you and you're wearing dirty underwear?" The new saying is "What if a car hits you and you're wearing underwear?"

I thought my brightly patterned bikini briefs were hip enough. At least I wasn't sporting the old white cotton numbers that could double as truce flags. But no. Now I'm a thong lady. Bonnie has me convinced that the backside V is synonymous with a woman who doesn't wash.

It's typical of the differences in a man's life and a woman's. A man is allowed to wear boxer shorts that tickle his knees. A woman has to wear a slingshot.

Having sorted out my bottom half with Lucille's miracle garment and the slingshot, I was next in search of a strapless bra that offered support; so many of the dresses that are available to women today fail to take into account the breast factor. I again deferred to Lucille's expertise and her suggestion of a convertible bra.

"You just remove the back of this strap, extend it, hook it to the top of the other side, and voilà — a one-shouldered bra,"

261

Lucille instructed.

"Let me try it."

"It's easy," Lucille said, closing the dressing room door. "Call me if you need any help."

I attempted to follow the same steps Lucille had so carefully explained to me. I fastened and unfastened and fastened again. I extended one arm through one hole and avoided the other. I hooked the back and turned hopefully to the mirror. I had fashioned what could only be described as a strapless noose sling.

"Help . . . Lucille . . . I'm choking," I coughed out.

Lucille did not respond. She was evidently strangling another customer.

I went to work at repositioning my bra straps. In a movement worthy of Houdini, I unhooked the back, grabbed one strap with my teeth, and forced my head underneath an opening to win my freedom. Like my husband appearing in the kitchen after all the dishes have been done and asking, "Anything I can do?" Lucille appeared in the dressing room and asked, "Need any help?"

"No, I don't need help. However, I do think I need a lawyer."

I abandoned the convertible bra and

decided to try something Bonnie had recommended to me that I had studiously been avoiding: the sticky bra. This bra was a risk because there was no way to try it on. You just had to buy it and hope it stuck.

Unpacking it at home, I became trepidatious when I saw the instruction booklet and the bottle of glue. I wasn't putting together a model airplane; I was trying to wear a bra. There was no turning back. I had cut the box open, and the *This Item Is Not Returnable* label decorated the front of the package with the obviousness of a cigarette health warning.

Wash your skin thoroughly before using this product. Do not swallow. If rash occurs see a doctor. I forged on. I applied the glue under my left breast. I let it go for the briefest of seconds so I could pick up the corresponding cup. My breast stuck to the skin beneath it. I grabbed for the instructions and turned to the troubleshooting section.

If breast becomes stuck to skin beneath, gently pry apart, using soap and water if necessary. I pried and soaped and began again, this time not letting it go. I positioned the cup and reached for the instructions.

Hold in place until secure.

Never mentioning how long this would take seemed to me to be a crucial bit of missing information. I slowly removed my hand. Things were still moving.

Twenty minutes later, with both breasts glued into place, I carefully slipped into my slingshot and shimmied into my miracle garment. I stepped into my ultra-tight strapless dress, proving I could fit into it. I was then ready to go out to dinner with my husband and not eat anything until we arrived back home.

I am my mother.

I worry about being an older mother, but I guess we'll just connect in different ways. We'll both be losing our teeth at around the same time.

Speak Up

One of the many things that's become more complicated in my fifty-plus years is sound. Maybe it's a tender-gender issue, but do you know what sentence I've never heard a woman say? "It's time to update my speaker system."

I know lots of different types of women, and not one of them has ever felt the need for a subwoofer.

When I was single (and boy, was I single . . . I wasn't even allowed to chew Doublemint gum) I had a $99 stereo system that came with two petite speakers. I kept them side by side in the front of the living room.

Whenever a man would venture into my life, one of the first things he would say was, "Why do you have your speakers together? Why don't you separate them? You're missing out on the whole concept of the stereo experience."

I had them positioned together for a good reason. I liked the sound to be in front of me. I lived in New York; I didn't want anyone singing at me from behind the couch. It made me nervous then, and it makes me nervous today. When I'm in a movie theater and I hear footsteps running on the ceiling in the back-right-hand corner of the auditorium, I automatically reach for my pepper spray.

Last year my husband decided our stereo system was out of step with our lifestyle.

"We hardly ever listen to music at home, and whenever we do, the phone rings and we have to turn it off," I argued.

"Exactly. That's why I've ordered the phone interrupter. When the phone rings the music will automatically cut out. You're going to love it. I'm having speakers installed in all four walls in the living room. We can have the radio on all day."

There you have it: a man who seldom listens to anything I say wanted to hear strangers talk to him from four different angles.

"You should have decided to do this before you moved in. It would have been much easier," the stereo expert explained, stating something so obvious even our goldfish rolled her eyes. "Do you still have this color paint?" he asked, pointing to the gash he had made on the wall.

"Sure," my husband answered, not taking into account that it wasn't paint but Venetian plaster that had taken approximately ten days of layering and five layers of scraping.

"I'll have to cut some holes in the bathrooms and the television room," he commented, dollar signs appearing in his pupils.

"Not the television room! Nothing will ever again be drilled in the television room," I cried out. (Please refer to "Television Envy" to comprehend the intensity of my response.)

"Rita, you don't understand. This will increase the resale value of our apartment."

"Are we moving and you haven't told me?"

"I'm just thinking ahead," my husband replied. "People like powerful stereo systems. They have big parties and they like to play music."

"Who are we going to sell the apartment to? P. Diddy?"

The stereo expert turned to me.

"You're making a mistake. You'll look back and wish you had speakers in the television room."

"I don't look back. I'm like a shark — I

only look forward."

By reverting to that old familiar female tactic, crying, I got my way and holes were eventually drilled in every room in the house except the television room. Holes were also added to our balconies so our upstairs and downstairs neighbors could enjoy our choice of music as well. I wondered how our stereo system would affect their resale value.

A week later, the stereo components in place, the speakers inserted into the holes, and paint carefully applied to mask the wounds perpetrated on the walls, my husband summoned me, our baby, and our dog into the living room.

"Listen to this," he crowed.

He twisted a knob on the wall and out burst a track from *The Best of Van Halen.* The sofa began to vibrate, the dog ran out of the room, the baby burst into tears, and the phone rang almost immediately. The music ceased, courtesy of the phone interrupter.

"It works," my husband exclaimed, picking up the receiver. "My phone interrupter works."

"No, no," he said into the receiver. "We're all right . . . No, the building isn't exploding . . . No, we won't have it that loud again. My wife just wanted to test the system. Sorry about that. You have a nice nap."

"Who was that?"

"Our upstairs neighbor. Plastic Lady. She bothers me too. I don't tell her to get breasts that match."

"Well, at least we know the phone interrupter works and we can play music, but maybe just not as loud," I said reassuringly, attempting to make the best of the situation.

"That's negating the whole stereo experience," he said.

"We'll always have the resale value," I added.

"Not without the speakers in the television room." Tears appeared in the corners of his eyes.

"All right, you can have the speakers in the television room," I acquiesced, walking out of the room.

The speakers were installed in the television room, begging the question of why anyone would sit in the television room and listen to the stereo. Isn't hindsight annoying?

We haven't used the updated stereo system recently, but we do turn it on from time to time just to make sure it works. And if Mr.

Diddy ever wants to move to Las Vegas, do
we have an apartment for him!

My husband won't let me sunbathe topless. He says he's afraid I might poke someone's knee out.

SHAKE, RATTLE, AND REBUILD

There have been few things more frightening in my life than the 1994 California earthquake. I'd been through tremors before and thought they were kind of exciting. They consisted of a gentle roll followed by a startled look followed by the question "Was that an earthquake?"

Because tremors had been our only earthquake experience, we had no qualms about buying a four-story house perched on the top of a hill. Then at about four in the morning, while we were sleeping soundly in our newly purchased bed in our newly purchased house, a jolt tossed us both up into the air. The whole house swayed violently. I still remember opening my eyes, seeing the wood beams on our cathedral ceiling, and thinking, *This is how I'm going to die.*

Some people wake up and their brain begins functioning immediately. I am not one of those people. I need a cup of coffee and ten minutes of staring into space to enter the world in which we are all trying to live.

Martin is good in a major crisis; when our world is crumbling around us, he keeps his cool and thinks logically. I'm good in a minor crisis; if I run out of sugar when I'm making a cake, I can go to the supermarket and buy some more.

I know the quake only lasted about seven seconds, but it felt like an hour. Our bedroom, located on the top floor of our four-story home, incurred the most sway. To understand what I'm talking about, hold a long blade of grass in the air and wave it from side to side. We were the two people positioned on the tip of the grass.

"I'll get a flashlight," Martin announced as we were still being flipped by the force of the earth like onions in a pan. Earthquake virgins, we had not positioned the flashlight at the side of the bed, where everyone had told us to keep it, but in a drawer located in the closet. The door had separated from the closet and was blocking the entrance. (An earthquake tells you exactly how many nails a builder has used to hold your house together. Our builder turned out to be a minimalist.)

Martin doesn't wear pajamas, so he had a very special incentive to get into the closet because that is where his robe lived. In the back recesses of my mind I remembered the advice to stand in a doorway. I stood in the doorway, effectively blocking Martin's path to the closet. Another rumble shook me to one side, and my husband climbed over me and the severed door and quickly located his robe and flashlight.

"We're still alive. We're still alive," I kept mumbling as we headed for the stairs. I saw the chandelier above the stairwell swaying like we were on the *Titanic.* We'd bought a house and we were on a ship.

We bolted out of the front door and joined our sleepy, shocked neighbors standing in the middle of the road.

Since we had only moved in a few weeks before, we had not really had a chance to get to know anyone, but we now knew our neighbor across the street rather well because she was naked.

"I didn't have a chance to grab any clothes," she explained as she attempted and failed to cover herself strategically.

Just then a man ran out of the house carrying a blanket. Our neighbor gratefully clutched the wrap to her body.

"Are you all right?" I asked the woman.

"I'm fine, and I wanted to tell you I really liked *Peter's Friends*." (*Peter's Friends* was a movie Martin and I had recently written.)

"Thank you," I replied.

We were definitely in Hollywood. We'd all just shared a near-death experience, and my naked neighbor was flattering me about our movie.

I noticed a smell of booze permeating the air. It turns out that in an earthquake not only do you find out how many nails a builder has used to put your house together, you also find out how much alcohol your neighbors' houses contain. There was wine to the left of us and hard liquor to the right. I inhaled sharply. I needed a drink.

Martin and I had just splurged on our dream house. All of our available cash had been put up as a down payment and we had assumed a massive mortgage. Tears filled my eyes as I witnessed the cracked walls and the French doors lying on the ground of our front patio.

"Well, we bought a new house and now we own a fixer-upper," Martin commented.

The earthquake had happened not even ten minutes before and Martin had made the first joke.

The good news for us was that our house was still standing. The inspector assured us that the foundation to our house was intact and the damage was merely cosmetic. Our naked neighbor's house had to be torn down and totally rebuilt.

The damage our house sustained was, however, substantial. The kitchen looked like a Greek wedding; every glass had been thrown into the center island and had smashed. The refrigerator doors had flown off and the fridge's contents were slathered across the floor. Imagine if Jackson Pollock had painted with mayonnaise, eggs, and milk.

Upstairs, the cabinets had been tossed across the bathroom, and in the bedroom the brand-new television was facedown on the floor, surrounded by Martin's extensive book collection.

"It'll be OK," Martin comforted. "We have earthquake insurance."

We did. Our earthquake insurance covered the contents of our refrigerator. We were reimbursed eighty-five dollars.

The earthquake was over, but the aftershocks continued. Every time we had the cracks in the walls replastered, the earth would rejiggle and the cracks would open up again like burst surgical stitches. Eventually we decided that our handyman had made enough money out of us and it was cheaper to consider the cracks as deliberate. They also served as a reminder of what could happen.

Fifteen years later, even though we no longer live in Los Angeles, Martin and I still sleep with flashlights and robes on either side of our bed. In case of emergency, we want to be able to see where we're going. And if we end up standing outside at four in the morning, we'd prefer not to be naked.

My aunt Sylvie is getting a neck lift, a breast lift, and a knee lift. Her surgeon is having a special: "All You Can Lift."

Who Don't You Trust?

As I've grown older, I've realized that I've learned as much from my father's bad behavior as I did from his good. It always bothered me that he had no friends. In order to have friends, an essential trust in human nature must exist. I think my father would have happily stayed in his mother's womb forever because no one could get in to steal anything.

I remember as an adolescent having to turn on all the lights and turn up the radio volume when we left the house so we wouldn't be robbed, and having to keep the lights and television on low when we were home so we wouldn't be killed.

Once I came home from shopping with my friends an hour early. I rang the doorbell repeatedly but there was no answer. I knew my father was home, so I called through the locked window, "Dad, open the door." Nothing. I went next door and called him.

280

He answered the phone.

"Dad, it's me."

"Don't come near the house," he warned. "There's a crazy lady ringing the doorbell and shouting, 'Dad, open the door.' "

"Yes, that would be me."

"It's only three o'clock. You said you'd be home at four."

"It's still me, even if it's three o'clock. You have to make the adjustment."

My father was overly suspicious of everyone and everything. He stopped eating in his favorite cafeteria because he didn't like the way the turkey carver looked at him when he held the knife. He retained a post office box because he didn't want the mailman to know where he lived.

I remember one phone conversation during which my father informed me that his new neighbor was a prostitute.

"What makes you think that?" I asked.

"Every weekend there's a different car parked in her driveway and they stay for a few hours and then they leave," he replied.

"She's not a prostitute. She has friends."

"She lets them into the house?"

"Yes, some people actually let other people into their homes," I informed him.

"That's just crazy."

After my stepmother died, my father

would not even let a cleaning person into the house. He had a vague memory of a lawyer he knew being accused of sexual misconduct by a housekeeper, and so he would never be alone with a woman in any situation without witnesses. Even when staying in a hotel, the maid would not be allowed in to clean his room for his entire stay.

I'd say, "Dad, put the Do Not Disturb sign up when you're in and let her clean when you go out. Why is that not acceptable?"

"I don't want anybody stealing anything either."

"I've stayed in hotel rooms for years and the housekeepers have never taken anything."

"I'm not saying it's them. I've seen what happens. The maids leave the doors open. They block the doorway with the cart and anyone can move it while they're cleaning the bathroom and come in and rob you blind."

"What is it that you have to steal that's so valuable? Socks? Underwear?"

"You're joking, but they're of very good quality."

"Then put them in the safe."

That was only the tip of my father's

paranoia. The bartender was slipping mickeys into his martinis (he'd had too much to drink and fallen asleep in the lounge). The man across the street was running a drug cartel (he was moving in). After an argument with my stepmother he threw away his mouthwash, suspecting she had tampered with it (she had loosened the cap on the bottle for him because she knew he was incapable).

Bizarrely, the same man who rampantly mistrusted innocent people placed complete trust in a person who was ripping him off. A painter quoted him $7,000 to fix a small portion of his roof. Without getting a second opinion, my father paid it. The same workman pointed out that the entire roof needed to be resealed for another $11,000 and my father didn't blink. I don't know what else this man spotted that needed thousands of dollars' worth of attention because my father stopped telling me once I threatened to intervene and question the painter as to exactly the nature of the work he was performing.

"This guy Hank, he's a hell of a painter," my father would insist. "He's a hell of a nice guy too. He brings me coffee every morning from 7-Eleven. Nobody's ever brought me coffee before."

I decided to let it go and let my father make his own mistakes. It was his money and I guess even a man as reclusive as my father occasionally needs a friend. After Hank ran out of fake home improvements he asked for money for a hernia operation. Then Hank disappeared, but my father remembered him fondly.

It saddens me to think of how many real friends my father could have remembered fondly if he had only trusted a tiny bit more.

I don't plan to grow old gracefully. I plan to have face-lifts until my ears meet.

MY DOG BONKERS

I'm a dog person. There is something about their hopeful faces and trusting eyes that I find totally irresistible. Often in a dog person's life there is one dog you connect with more than any other. I've had other dogs in my life. I raised them from puppyhood. When I was a child, I had a ridiculously loyal German shepherd that I named Tiny and when I was a teenager I had a cute but not too bright Afghan-poodle mix that I named Agatha. I loved them both dearly, but Bonkers, who came to me already named and whom I didn't meet until he was around two, was the dog that will always be with me.

There is really no way to tell what breed of dog he was. He looked like a cross between a bath mat and Kenny Rogers. I guess it was his good looks that got him noticed and plucked from a pound when he was a puppy to take part in a show called

Superdogs at the Excalibur Hotel and Casino in Las Vegas. This was an afternoon show where dogs from various shelters were loosely trained to run back and forth and jump over sticks.

We attended an afternoon performance of *Superdogs,* and that is where we first saw Bonkers jump through the hoop. He was magnificent. It was as if his back legs were springs. Bonkers was also the high jumper in the show. The final trick consisted of the emcee calling his name, and Bonkers running from behind the curtains and propelling himself over an impossibly high stick.

"That dog looks a little like my old dog Agatha," I whispered to Martin during the show.

"I've always wanted a dog," my husband replied. "My mother would never let me have one."

I filed Martin's request in an overstuffed back cubbyhole in my mind. Maybe one day we would get a dog. One day, but not now.

We enjoyed the show so much we attended it again the next week only to find that Bonkers was no longer a part of it.

"Maybe it's his day off," I reasoned. "Maybe he has friends coming into town and he needs to take them around sightseeing. After all, this is Vegas."

"Go backstage and ask what's happened to Bonkers," my husband commanded.

I located Ben, Bonkers's owner and the emcee of the show, and demanded to know what had happened to the shaggy star. The news was not good. Bonkers had been hit by a car and his back left leg had been shattered. He was being operated on at the moment and there was a chance he would not be able to walk again.

"We'll take him," my husband and I both said in unison.

"Wait until we see how he comes out of the operation," Ben suggested.

I phoned Ben once a week to check up on Bonkers's recuperation, and in eight weeks he was ready for us to pick him up and take him home.

Martin and I drove to Vegas to meet up with Ben. It was a little like a drug deal. Ben had told us to look for a white Honda Escort on the north side of the Excalibur parking lot, and he would be wearing a blue cap. We spotted the car and out popped Ben and a very skinny Bonkers. He had been shaved and a large scar now decorated his left back leg.

"He has a plate in his hip and a few teeth got knocked out in the accident, but I think he's going to be fine," Ben announced.

Bonkers was one lucky Vegas dog. He'd gone from a pound to being the star of a show to the brink of death to about to be sleeping on a pillow-topped mattress in Beverly Hills.

In no time at all, the bouncy dog we had seen in the show began to reemerge. Vestiges of his former show business life surfaced when we least expected it. Bonkers could be summoned into a room not by calling his name but by applause. Because "Happy Birthday" had been sung to kids in the audience he recognized the tune and would sing along. When friends came over we would occasionally bring out the hoop and Bonkers would instantly sail through it. He was an official member of the family and appeared on our Christmas card in various festive poses every year.

When I was once again booked to appear in Vegas we put Bonkers in the car and headed back to his homeland. Upon arriving at the hotel, we were told that no dogs were allowed on the premises and he would have to stay in a kennel. I was booked for two weeks, and that was quite simply unacceptable.

"Bonkers is in Rita's show," my husband, ever the problem-solving producer, lied.

"Oh, he's in the show. Then I guess we

could make an exception," the entertainment president replied. "But he's going to have to behave. Liza Minnelli snuck her Yorkie into the suite last week, and I don't want to go into detail, but we've had to order a new sofa. By the way, what exactly does Bonkers do?"

"You'll see," I replied mysteriously.

Bonkers was back in show business. I just had to figure out his talent. He was on that night, so I didn't have time to train him. I hadn't traveled with his hoop and I really didn't want to make him jump for a living. It was so undignified.

That evening I walked through the casino with a sixty-pound hairy hound and even the sober people were questioning what they saw. I deposited Bonkers in my dressing room, supplied him with a bowl of water and his favorite duckie toy, and told him to have a good show. I asked the stage manager to get Bonkers from my dressing room seventy minutes into my act and wait for me to call for him. I didn't know what he would do, but I did know that the entertainment president would be in the audience waiting for Bonkers to appear.

At the end of my act I announced to the audience, "I have a special treat for you tonight. Would you like to meet my dog,

Bonkers?"

"Yes!" was the resounding reply.

Phil, the stage manager, unleashed Bonkers, and he came bounding onto the stage.

"Sit," I commanded. Bonkers ignored me. "OK, don't sit," I ordered. He continued not sitting.

"See, ladies and gentlemen, he didn't sit." I had stumbled upon our act.

"Don't lie down," I told him. Again, success.

The audience applauded. Bonkers ran to the edge of the stage, his tail wagging wildly. I had another idea.

"Let's do some impressions. Bonkers, windshield wiper, windshield wiper," I commanded. His tail flailed back and forth wildly. "Helicopter, helicopter," I directed as I noticed his tail beginning to fly in circles. "Bark at the lady in the yellow dress in the front row," I said as he began to bark anyway.

I remembered the certain spot on Bonkers's back that made his back leg rotate. I scratched it.

"Start the motorcycle," I said as his back leg moved around in a circle. The audience was in hysterics, and I sensed it was time for the big finale.

"Be as tall as Mickey Rooney," I instructed as I patted my legs. Bonkers jumped up on my dress and I led him offstage to thunderous applause. Our act was born. Bonkers proceeded to perform in my show whenever I played Vegas for the next twelve years. He played seven different hotels and stayed in all the best suites, and they never once had to replace a sofa.

Aside from being a Vegas draw, Bonkers appeared on billboards advertising animal shelters and posters auctioning a motorcycle for charity. He was also polite. I taught him to say thank you when he was given his dinner, and he always tapped me on the leg lightly whenever he needed to go outside.

We were living in Las Vegas and Bonkers and I were performing at New York New York when it happened. My ever-hungry dog was carefully watching me eat spaghetti when he barked a bark I'd never heard before.

"What was that?" I asked my husband.

"I don't know," he replied worriedly.

Bonkers sat down and appeared dizzy. I said, "Bonkers, say thank you," a certain attention getter. He just stared.

I offered him some spaghetti and he turned it down. That had never happened before. We had just enough time to take him to the vet before I went to work that night.

The vet looked at his gums. They were pale. "This is serious. I'm going to have to keep him here," he warned.

"How could this happen? He was fine and then with one bark he's not fine. What's going on?"

"I'll run some tests and take some X-rays. Call me in a few hours."

My husband called the animal hospital later that night. The vet had stayed overtime trying to decipher what had gone wrong with our doggie. Martin listened on the phone quietly and shook his head, indicating things were not going well. He hung up the receiver.

"Dr. Wesley says he's got a tumor in his chest and his lungs were filled with water and we should call in the morning, but he thinks we might have to put him to sleep."

I had always thought that I would have time to prepare for this horrible moment, but life doesn't really care what you think. Out of the blue, my dog, my friend, and my co-star were all about to leave me. Martin called the animal hospital the next morning. Dr. Wesley had slept in the office that night to keep an eye on Bonkers. He was no better, but no worse. Martin couldn't tolerate me crying all the way to the animal hospital, so he decided to drive down and look at Bonkers himself before making the final decision. I waited by the phone.

"I'm bringing him home," my husband said. "He wagged his tail when he saw me, and I just have to bring him home . . . even if it's only for a few days."

Amazingly, Bonkers lived for two more years after that episode. He never performed again, but he did accompany me to the theater at least twice a week to visit his friends backstage. It wasn't an easy two years. I had a shelf in the kitchen I called "Bonkers's pharmacy," and his pill schedule was rigorous. Among various medications, he was on a high dose of diuretics, which meant he had to be walked every two hours. We live in a high-rise, so that was a challenge, but the upside was I didn't have to go to the gym. I just walked my dog twelve times a day. I don't know if we did the right thing in not putting him down when the vet advised it, but I do know I had my dog with me for two extra years, and although he was never young Bonkers again, he seemed happy.

My husband and I made a vow that if we ever felt he was suffering, we would have to be brave. One day I came into the bathroom, where Bonkers had been sleeping on his favorite rug, to take him for his walk, and he was having some sort of seizure. I called Martin and we knelt beside him and tried to calm him down. When Bonkers came to, he was panting heavily and appeared dizzy.

I showed him his leash and he looked away. He refused to move out of the bathroom. It was as if he was telling us he'd had enough.

We called our vet and he came to the house and gave our beloved dog a shot of morphine. The wild panting began to subside and Bonkers began to snore. It was a really great, deep snore, the kind of snore you snore when every bit of you is relaxed and you haven't a worry in the world. It was a truly wonderful noise. We wrapped Bonkers in one of my daughter's blankets and took him to the animal hospital to be put to sleep.

This is the first year in thirteen years that Bonkers will not be on our Christmas card. All of our friends know he's gone, but I know they'll be upset all the same. Some people would think that Bonkers got lucky when we saw him in the show and took him in after his car accident, but I think we were the ones who were really lucky, because he was our dog.

ENDGAME

Once you've finished a book, you then have to name it. This takes just as long as it did to write the book. The following are some of the titles that were under consideration. If there's one that you particularly prefer, please feel free to alter the front of this book accordingly. (Only do this if you have purchased the book. I would feel terrible if I was responsible for your arrest in a bookshop.)

Help! My Birthday Cake's on Fire
Aged to Imperfection
I'm Still Hot (It Just Comes in Flashes)
If Fifty Is the New Thirty, I'm Thirty-Three
I Won't Blog, Don't Ask Me
Artificially Hip
That Botox Has Sailed
I Remember James Taylor When He Had Hair

Half a Century Is Better than None
Ritalosophy
I'm Not Over the Hill — I Just Can't Climb It
350 in Dog Years
Suddenly Fifty
Older than Springtime, Younger than Angela Lansbury
I Remember What's-His-Name

ACKNOWLEDGMENTS

I'd like to thank my publisher, Shaye Areheart, for commissioning this book; my agent, Alan Nevins, for reminding Shaye that she'd commissioned this book, and my husband, Martin Bergman, for reminding me to write this book.

ABOUT THE AUTHOR

Rita Rudner is a celebrated and award-winning comedian, actress, screenwriter, presenter, and author. Past books include the bestselling *Naked Beneath My Clothes* and the novels *Tickled Pink* and *Turning the Tables.*

Writing this book would have been so much easier if I hadn't bought that ceiling computer.